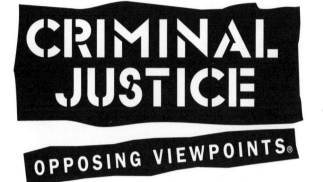

CRIMINAL JUSTICE

OPPOSING VIEWPOINTS®

Other Books of Related Interest in the Opposing Viewpoints Series:

CRIMINAL JUSTICE

OPPOSING VIEWPOINTS®

David Bender & Bruno Leone, *Series Editors*

Michael D. Biskup, *Book Editor*

OPPOSING
VIEWPOINTS
SERIES®

Greenhaven Press, Inc.   PO Box 289009   San Diego, CA 92198-9009

Library of Congress Cataloging-in-Publication Data

Criminal justice : opposing viewpoints / Michael D. Biskup, book editor.
      p.   cm. — (Opposing viewpoints series)
   Includes bibliographical references and index.
   Summary: presents opposing viewpoints on such aspects of criminal justice as reform of the system, rights of the accused, and police abuse of authority.
   ISBN 0-89908-624-1 (alk. paper) — ISBN 0-89908-623-3 (pbk. : alk. paper)
   1. Criminal justice, Administration of—United States. [1. Criminal justice, Administration of.] I. Biskup, Michael D., 1956-   . II. Series: Opposing viewpoints series (Unnumbered)
HV9950.C747 1993
364'.098'2468073—dc20   92-40709
                                                              CIP
                                                              AC

"Congress shall make no law . . . abridging the freedom of speech, or of the press."

First Amendment to the U.S. Constitution

The basic foundation of our democracy is the first amendment guarantee of freedom of expression. The Opposing Viewpoints Series is dedicated to the concept of this basic freedom and the idea that it is more important to practice it than to enshrine it.

Contents

Chapter 3: Should the Criminal Justice System Enforce Crime Victims' Rights?

Chapter 4: How Do Lawyers Affect the Criminal Justice System?

Chapter 5: Do Police Abuse Their Authority?

Why Consider Opposing Viewpoints?

"The only way in which a human being can make some approach to knowing the whole of a subject is by hearing what can be said about it by persons of every variety of opinion and studying all modes in which it can be looked at by every character of mind. No wise man ever acquired his wisdom in any mode but this."

John Stuart Mill

In our media-intensive culture it is not difficult to find differing opinions. Thousands of newspapers and magazines and dozens of radio and television talk shows resound with differing points of view. The difficulty lies in deciding which opinion to agree with and which "experts" seem the most credible. The more inundated we become with differing opinions and claims, the more essential it is to hone critical reading and thinking skills to evaluate these ideas. Opposing Viewpoints books address this problem directly by presenting stimulating debates that can be used to enhance and teach these skills. The varied opinions contained in each book examine many different aspects of a single issue. While examining these conveniently edited opposing views, readers can develop critical thinking skills such as the ability to compare and contrast authors' credibility, facts, argumentation styles, use of persuasive techniques, and other stylistic tools. In short, the Opposing Viewpoints Series is an ideal way to attain the higher-level thinking and reading skills so essential in a culture of diverse and contradictory opinions.

In addition to providing a tool for critical thinking, Opposing Viewpoints books challenge readers to question their own strongly held opinions and assumptions. Most people form their opinions on the basis of upbringing, peer pressure, and personal, cultural, or professional bias. By reading carefully balanced opposing views, readers must directly confront new ideas as well as the opinions of those with whom they disagree. This is not to simplistically argue that everyone who reads opposing views will—or should—change his or her opinion. Instead, the series enhances readers' depth of understanding of their own views by encouraging confrontation with opposing ideas. Careful examination of others' views can lead to the readers' understanding of the logical inconsistencies in their own opinions, perspective on why they hold an opinion, and the consideration of the possibility that their opinion requires further evaluation.

Evaluating Other Opinions

To ensure that this type of examination occurs, Opposing Viewpoints books present all types of opinions. Prominent spokespeople on different sides of each issue as well as well-known professionals from many disciplines challenge the reader. An additional goal of the series is to provide a forum for other, less known, or even unpopular viewpoints. The opinion of an ordinary person who has had to make the decision to cut off life support from a terminally ill relative, for example, may be just as valuable and provide just as much insight as a medical ethicist's professional opinion. The editors have two additional purposes in including these less known views. One, the editors encourage readers to respect others' opinions—even when not enhanced by professional credibility. It is only by reading or listening to and objectively evaluating others' ideas that one can determine whether they are worthy of consideration. Two, the inclusion of such viewpoints encourages the important critical thinking skill of objectively evaluating an author's credentials and bias. This evaluation will illuminate an author's reasons for taking a particular stance on an issue and will aid in readers' evaluation of the author's ideas.

As series editors of the Opposing Viewpoints Series, it is our hope that these books will give readers a deeper understanding of the issues debated and an appreciation of the complexity of even seemingly simple issues when good and honest people disagree. This awareness is particularly important in a democratic society such as ours in which people enter into public debate to determine the common good. Those with whom one disagrees should not be regarded as enemies but rather as people whose views deserve careful examination and may shed light on one's own.

Thomas Jefferson once said that "difference of opinion leads to inquiry, and inquiry to truth." Jefferson, a broadly educated man, argued that "if a nation expects to be ignorant and free . . . it expects what never was and never will be." As individuals and as a nation, it is imperative that we consider the opinions of others and examine them with skill and discernment. The Opposing Viewpoints Series is intended to help readers achieve this goal.

David L. Bender & Bruno Leone,
Series Editors

Introduction

"Better that many guilty shall go free rather than one innocent should suffer."

John Adams

The protection of those accused of crime has been of fundamental importance since the founding of the United States. The idea that allowing even the guilty to go free if it may protect one innocent person from conviction is regarded by many as a high ideal for which our criminal justice system must continually strive. Concurrently, a growing number of people believe that the victim of crime is sacrificed to this ideal. It is the rights of these victims, critics of the system argue, that must be of paramount consideration.

Concern for the rights of the victim has been translated into legal action in many states. Victims' legal rights have been expanded to include the right to be kept informed of all proceedings regarding their case, including preliminary hearings, plea bargaining efforts, and police investigations. Many states have established victim compensation programs, and, if the accused is convicted, some states allow the victim to participate in the parole hearings. Most controversially, the right to be present and to testify at the trial has been enlarged to include the family members of murder victims, even when they were not witnesses to the crime. Typically, they testify to the extreme trauma the murder has caused their family in an attempt to plead with the court to bring justice for the family member's death.

These changes have altered the way police, lawyers, judges, and others in the criminal justice system view both the victim and the accused. While this shift in focus from the accused to the victim is heralded as a much-needed improvement by many, others worry that it will greatly diminish the rights of the accused. After all, the myriad of legal rights the accused now have at their disposal were not granted readily, but were fought for and won because many people perceived a need for such reforms. Laws like *Miranda*, in which the accused must be informed of his or her rights, are a good example. *Miranda*'s original intent was to deter and control police power by limiting unauthorized searches and interrogations. Other rights, like plea bargaining, the right to appeal a conviction, and the right to be represented by an attorney even if one cannot afford one, are guarantees many people in our society applaud. However, there have always been those who criticize these protections as excessive and who argue that they allow hardened criminals to manipulate the system and escape punishment. This view seems to be gathering momentum as the victim continues gaining public sympathy and judicial support.

Whether or not the victim's increased role is positive, it represents a major shift from John Adams's ideal—a distanced and rational system of justice—to one where personal emotions like sympathy, anger, and even vengeance come into play. Will a murdered child's mother testifying before the court have such impact upon the jury that the jury will ignore the evidence? Is the courtroom becoming a battleground, where the jury is asked to take retribution and exact a type of tribal justice rather than base its decision on the facts and presentation of the case itself?

Throughout *Criminal Justice: Opposing Viewpoints* the rights of the victim and of the accused appear to be in continual conflict. The five topics debated are: What Reforms Would Improve the Criminal Justice System? Do the Rights of the Accused Undermine the Criminal Justice System? Should the Criminal Justice System Enforce Crime Victims' Rights? How Do Lawyers Affect the Criminal Justice System? Do Police Abuse Their Authority? The viewpoints in these chapters reflect the ongoing debate concerning how the United States can provide justice for all of its citizens.

What Reforms Would Improve the Criminal Justice System?

CRIMINAL JUSTICE

Chapter Preface

The symbol for justice is a figure of a blindfolded woman holding scales in one hand and a sword in the other. The scales represent weighing the evidence on each side of a dispute, the sword symbolizes administering justice swiftly once a decision has been made, and the blindfold indicates rendering a decision without favoring either side. Yet, many political cartoons depict a more beleaguered justice: Her blindfold is falling, her scales are tipped, or her sword is falling out of her hand. These cartoons reflect the overwhelming view that justice in America is difficult to achieve, and that the criminal justice system, in particular, needs reform.

Critics of the criminal justice system agree that overburdened courtrooms, delayed trials, and predominately white judges, lawyers, and juries unfairly decide the fate of minority defendants. They contend that overcrowded prisons and misinterpreted constitutional rights prevent courts from sending all of the guilty to prison. Finally, they see a system that favors the rich, neglects victims, and places a priority on procedure rather than on determining guilt or innocence. Many legal experts and lay people believe the legal system has lost touch with its original intent: to dispense justice equitably and swiftly.

The vastness of the criminal justice system, the complexity of some of its problems, and the sheer number of changes needed to reform it seem overwhelming. The authors in the following chapter offer possible solutions for creating a criminal justice system that lives up to the ideal represented by the symbol of justice.

"Racism continues to haunt our judicial system."

Eliminate Racism to Improve Criminal Justice

The National Association for the Advancement of Colored People Legal Defense and Education Fund

In 1991 four white Los Angeles police officers beat an African-American man named Rodney King after they stopped him for speeding. At a criminal trial, an all-white jury acquitted the four men of the beating. The verdict sparked numerous riots in Los Angeles in reaction to what African-Americans perceived as an injustice. In the following article, the National Association for the Advancement of Colored People (NAACP) Legal Defense and Education Fund contends that this incident is symptomatic of racism in the American judicial system. The author argues that having more African-American jurors and judges would eliminate the racist attitudes within the system. The New York City-based fund works to end discrimination in the criminal justice system.

As you read, consider the following questions:

1. Why do most African-Americans perceive the American criminal justice system as racist, according to the author?
2. What are five reforms that would help improve the criminal justice system, according to the author?
3. According to the author, what can be done to increase the number of African-American judges in both elected and appointed jurisdictions?

The National Association for the Advancement of Colored People Legal Defense and Education Fund, "The Color of Justice," *ABA Journal* 78 (August 1992): 62-63. Copyright © 1992 by the American Bar Association. Reprinted by permission of the *ABA Journal*.

The acquittal of the Los Angeles police officers who brutalized Rodney King was a stark reminder that racism continues to haunt our judicial system—a racial discrimination that it is imperative for America to acknowledge.

Denied Equal Justice

But it is equally important to understand that the anger ignited by this verdict among African-Americans was based on the well-founded belief that people of color are consistently denied equal justice in our courts. (A recent poll shows that 81 percent of African-Americans believe that the judicial system is racially biased.)

In the Rodney King case, the first assault on simple justice was, of course, the beating itself. The second occurred when this racially charged case was moved to a nearly all-white community. That change of venue had precisely the same discriminatory effect as practices that were once used to exclude African-Americans from juries when Jim Crow ruled much of this land.

The final assault on justice was the verdict. The jurors, none of whom were African-American, apparently were unable to see a person of color like King as anything other than a threat, as opposed to a helpless human being who was mauled by officers of the law.

The jury accepted the astonishing proposition that 17 police officers could not contain or handcuff King unless four of them repeatedly beat him; and that something not seen on the videotape must have justified that beating. But it is simply unfathomable that King could have said and done anything that could justify such an abuse of power.

While outrageous, the verdict and the racism that infected it were hardly aberrations. Indeed, the perception among many African-Americans that there are two systems of justice—one for whites and one for people of color—is not a result of one jury's decision in Simi Valley.

Concrete Steps

That perception is based on a host of racial inequities in our legal system—a system that is administered almost exclusively by whites, is designed primarily to protect white lives and white property, and assigns minimal value to the life and safety of an African-American like Rodney King.

A majority of Americans condemned the King verdict as well as the violence that occurred in its aftermath. Now, armed with an understanding of this astonishing verdict and the judicial system that made it possible, America must take concrete steps to remove race discrimination from our legal system:

• First, we must deal forthrightly with the problem of the exclusion of people of color from decision-making positions in our systems of justice—on both state and federal levels.

Of the nearly 12,000 full-time state court judges across the country, only 465 were African-American and 150 were Latino in 1991. Some states, like Texas, brazenly continue to elect their judges under election schemes that have been found by federal courts to discriminate against African-Americans and Latinos.

Rich white justice   Poor black justice

Paul Conrad, © 1990, *Los Angeles Times*. Reprinted with permission.

In the federal system, the White House seemingly has adopted the same criteria for courts of appeals positions that many private country clubs use to select members. No African-American sits on six federal appeals courts that have jurisdiction over 24 states.

It is little wonder that African-Americans have little confidence in the capacity of our courts to dispense color-blind justice. What is needed is a serious commitment by states that elect judges to abolish electoral schemes that prevent people of color from electing their representatives of choice. Equally important is an affirmative effort by the federal government and states that appoint judges to put more people of color on the judicial benches.

Legislative Reform

• Second, African-Americans have to be given an equal opportunity to serve as jurors. In too many cases, people of color continue to be peremptorily struck from juries by prosecutors. Prosecutors routinely remove large numbers of minority jurors because present law requires only that they provide a "race-neutral" reason for the removal.

But prosecutors can use a virtually unlimited number of reasons for striking minority jurors that appear to be race-neutral, even if the race of those jurors was foremost on their minds. For example, jurors who "look like the defendant," or "are the same age as the defendant," have been successfully removed. African-Americans are also routinely removed from juries in civil cases.

We must deal with this problem through legislation. Statutes allowing the removal of jurors only for case-related reasons will go a long way toward restoring the faith of African-Americans that people of color are equal participants in our justice system.

• Third, in racially charged cases, changes of venue cannot have the effect of excluding people of color. Those cases that arise in jurisdictions populated by substantial numbers of people of color should be moved only when it is clearly shown that the removal is necessary to ensure a fair trial. And they should be moved only to communities with comparable ethnic or racial characteristics. This problem can be solved by legislation.

• Fourth, eliminating police brutality against people of color must become a national priority. The time has come for all communities to insist on civilian review of complaints of police misconduct and the active, independent prosecution of legitimate claims of police abuse. Police departments must take responsibility for implementing policies on the proper, restrained and non-racist use of force, and officers must be regularly retrained to ensure that those policies are not merely empty promises to people of color. Finally, all police departments in America need to provide racial sensitivity training.

Sentencing Reform

• Fifth, racial disparities in sentencing must end. A 1990 report from the General Accounting Office found that racial disparities in sentencing exist throughout the country. For much of our history, our judicial system has operated to value white lives more than black lives, and to punish more harshly those who commit crimes against whites.

Bias in sentencing is most clearly seen in capital sentencing. It is well established that those who kill whites are far more likely to receive the death penalty than are those who kill African-Americans. Congress has considered yet failed to pass the Fairness in Sentencing Act, a bill that would require state officials to show that the death penalty was not administered in a discriminatory manner. Its passage is long overdue.

Fostering the inclusion of people of color in the legal system and taking other steps to promote color-blind justice will help to ensure that equal justice for all is a reality to millions of citizens.

> *"The indigent criminal defendant seeking access to justice faces monumental barriers."*

Improve Services for Poor Defendants

Stephen J. Schulhofer

In 1963, the Supreme Court ruled in *Gideon v. Wainwright* that every criminal defendant has a right to have an attorney. As a result of this ruling, court-appointed attorneys known as public defenders usually defend the poor. In the following viewpoint, Stephen J. Schulhofer contends that lack of minimum attorney standards, low pay, and poorly staffed offices force lawyers to give substandard representation to poor clients. He argues that improving services for the poor would make the system more just. Schulhofer is a professor at the University of Chicago Law School and director of the school's Center for Studies in Criminal Justice.

As you read, consider the following questions:

1. What is the drawback to having a court appoint attorneys, according to Schulhofer?
2. According to the author, why is it difficult for a criminal defendant to challenge the competence of a court-appointed attorney?
3. What does Schulhofer suggest be done to improve indigent defender services?

From Stephen J. Schulhofer, "Access to Justice for the American Underclass." This article appeared in the June 1991 issue and is reprinted with permission from *The World & I*, a publication of The Washington Times Corporation, © 1991.

Prior to the Warren Court revolution of the 1960s, indigents had no constitutional right to counsel in noncapital felony cases, and many states either refused to appoint counsel or provided only perfunctory systems of representation. All this changed with the Supreme Court's *Gideon v. Wainwright* decision in 1963. Indigent criminal defendants now have an automatic right to appointed counsel in all felony cases and in any misdemeanor case in which imprisonment is imposed.

Part of the Picture

The existence of the indigent's constitutional right to counsel has revolutionized legal representation for the poor. Haphazard systems of trial without counsel and last-minute appointment of courthouse regulars have given way in many jurisdictions to large organizations of well-trained and dedicated public defenders. In Philadelphia, for example, the Defender Association's professional staff, on the eve of *Gideon,* consisted of only six attorneys. By 1967, the association employed thirty-six attorneys, ten investigators, and a social worker, and by 1984 its personnel included more than one hundred full-time attorneys and a substantial professional support staff.

These successes are only part of the picture, however. Implementation of the *Gideon* principle has been uneven, and there have been serious problems and disappointments. In part the disappointments stem from grudging judicial interpretation.

Although the Supreme Court acknowledges that the constitutionally required counsel must provide *effective* assistance, court decisions have provided only halfhearted enforcement of the requirement of effectiveness. Once certified as a member of the bar, counsel is presumed to be effective. The Court has held that neither gross inexperience nor unfamiliarity with criminal practice is enough to support a finding of ineffectiveness. And the courts have refused to mandate even the most elementary steps in effective case preparation, such as interviewing the client or witnesses. Instead, the courts judge ineffectiveness under the totality of the circumstances in each case.

This totality approach gives no guidance to the bar or to the states about proper expectations for defense counsel's performance. In individual cases, it is difficult to determine after trial, on the basis of a cold record, what more thorough investigation or preparation might have accomplished. In one case, Judge Henry Friendly, writing for the U.S. Court of Appeals for the Second Circuit, held that a lawyer was not ineffective even though he had slept through a portion of a witness's cross-examination. Judge Friendly simply speculated that the witness's testimony probably was not very important because "if it had been, [the trial judge] would have awakened him."

As a result of this totality of the circumstances approach, perfunctory representation goes unchecked. Judge David Bazelon once estimated that half of the attorneys appearing in the District of Columbia criminal courts were incompetent. Chief Justice Warren Burger, from the opposite end of the political spectrum, has been similarly critical of performance by defense attorneys. Incompetence is overlooked because to do otherwise would bring the criminal justice system to a standstill.

Problems of Providing Defender Services

Why is the level of performance so disappointing? The answer to this question involves not only the shape of judicial precedent interpreting the *Gideon* mandate but, more importantly, the way in which defense services are organized and delivered. The question becomes one of sociology, politics, and, above all, economics.

Counsel for the indigent is appointed by the court, which either assigns representation to an organized public defender, or selects an attorney who is in private practice. There are important variations on these two basic systems. In most jurisdictions, the chief defender is appointed by the judges of the court or by some other municipal official. Sixty-three percent of local defender organizations are agencies of city or county government, including 23 percent that are agencies of the judiciary. In these circumstances, the defender's budget, management, and case processing policies are dependent on the very authorities that the public defender is expected to challenge aggressively. Only about a third of the big-city defender associations have independent boards of directors.

There is a similar problem in the assignment of counsel from the private bar. The better approach, followed in many jurisdictions, is to draw the names of counsel at random from an established roster, or to have an independent bar association committee make selections. Often, however, judges assign attorneys personally, and the appointment power can easily be used to reward attorneys for cooperation and to deny business to those perceived as too aggressive.

The economics of indigent defense poses a distinct set of problems. Consider first the situation of appointed counsel. In some jurisdictions, appointed attorneys are involuntarily conscripted from the list of those admitted to the bar. Sometimes such attorneys are required to serve *pro bono publico*, donating whatever time it proves necessary (in *their* judgment) to give.

Some courts, recognizing the obvious connection between economics and the incentives for vigorous effort, have ordered states and counties to improve their compensation systems. But others have remained astonishingly insensitive to this problem. Chief Justice Joseph Weintraub once wrote for the New Jersey

Supreme Court, "A lawyer needs no motivation beyond his *sense of duty* and his *pride.*" Overall, only about half the jurisdictions considering this problem have found it impermissible to force attorneys to serve pro bono. The others view this obligation as a legitimate price for the privilege of practicing law.

Poor Salaries

It is revealing that courts focus primarily on whether the "pro bono" system is fair *to the attorney!* Most of the decisions gave scant attention to the devastating impact of this practice on the indigent's right to a dedicated and vigorous defense.

Fortunately, most jurisdictions do provide appointed attorneys some compensation. But the economic incentives remain skewed. One method of payment is the flat fee per case. This system poses an obvious threat to effective representation because the attorney has every incentive to minimize the time and effort spent on the case. Only about 10 percent of the counties that use an assigned counsel system still limit compensation to a flat fee.

Guaranteed Rights

The Sixth Amendment right to counsel was generally understood as guaranteeing criminal defendants the right to hire their own counsel if they could afford to do so. The Supreme Court has since ruled, however, that the Sixth Amendment right to counsel further requires that, in both federal cases (Johnson vs. Zerbst, 1938) and state cases (Gideon vs. Wainwright, 1963), the government must provide counsel to represent criminal defendants who cannot afford to hire counsel on their own, and that the right to counsel is guaranteed regardless of how short the defendant's term of imprisonment may be if convicted (Argersinger vs. Hamlin, 1972).

Warren Burger, *The Washington Times*, December 22, 1991.

The better and more common system is one of compensation on an hourly basis. In the federal system, appointed attorneys receive $40 to $60 per hour, and many states authorize compensation of about $40 or (less frequently) $50 per hour. Even at these rates, compensation for the appointed attorney can be quite modest in practice, since, as a Kansas court recently estimated, overhead expenses alone can range from $27 to $35 per hour.

In any event, the more typical practice is to set very low hourly rates. A survey completed by the Spangenberg Group revealed that as of 1990, authorized hourly rates for noncapital felonies (usually started at different levels for time spent out of court or in court) were $20 and $40 in Alabama; $30 in Illinois, Indiana, Michigan, and Washington; $25 and $35 in Kentucky, Louisiana, Massachusetts, and Wisconsin; and $20 and $30 in Mississippi, Montana, and Tennessee. In South Carolina, where a state task force proposed raising the rate to $40, the fee in effect under a 1982 statute is only $10 and $15 per hour. And in Connecticut, the authorized rate of compensation is $12.50 per hour.

The reality of indigent defense through an appointed attorney is even more dismal than these low hourly rates suggest. Most jurisdictions impose a cap on the total compensation that the defense attorney can be paid per case. The maximum for a felony case is $3,500 in the federal courts, and even this limitation can be waived by the chief judge. But in many states the applicable caps are quite low—$500 in North Carolina, Oklahoma, South Carolina, and Tennessee; $575 in Virginia; $1,000 in Alabama, Louisiana, Mississippi, and Vermont; and $1,200 in New York. . . .

Underfunded and Ineffective

The best hope for avoiding the skewed incentives of underfunded appointment systems is reliance on an organized defender agency. Defenders working on an annual salary probably have no immediate financial incentive to cut corners or dampen the vigor of their efforts. Some defender offices, most notably those in Washington, D.C., and Philadelphia, are staffed by well-trained, dedicated lawyers, and they render excellent service.

But most defender offices are woefully underfunded. Many, such as the Legal Aid Society of New York, are swamped by a staggering caseload. Inevitably, the top priority under such conditions is the need to move cases along. So in one form or another the pressure to cut corners, to stint on investigation and preparation, reemerges. No matter how dedicated, a defender with twenty-five to thirty cases to process in one day cannot provide thorough, vigorous representation.

Aggregate expenditure figures provide one measure of our paltry commitment to defense of the poor. In 1986 the average expenditure on indigent defense was only $223 per case. The *most* generous state, New Jersey, spent only $540 per case, and expenditure figures ranged downward from there, to a low of a mere $63 per case in Arkansas.

In theory, the constitutional right to effective assistance remains as a safeguard to correct the worst cases of inadequate representation. But as we have seen, the doctrines defining ineffective assistance are so vague that they seldom afford a viable source of protection. And there is another problem: How can the indigent defendant, most often a person of limited education and limited verbal skills, challenge the competence of the attorney appointed to represent him?

An Unfulfilled Promise

In most cities, 80% of criminal defendants are poor. . . . Big-city public defenders often must handle 15 to 20 felony cases in a single day. Many are skillful and do their best under adverse conditions, but they are forced to render perfunctory service. Many are not so skillful. Low salaries for public defenders force rapid turnover, and court-appointed private practitioners in many states receive only $10 to $30 per hour, with a cap of $500 or $1,000 per case—often not even enough to cover overhead.

Stephen J. Schulhofer, *Los Angeles Times*, December 17, 1991.

The usual avenue for raising a constitutional claim of ineffective assistance is a separate proceeding filed after conviction. This postconviction proceeding provides a way to hold a hearing on issues related to the fairness of the original trial, issues (like ineffectiveness) that often could not be litigated at the time of the trial itself.

Monumental Barriers

The postconviction proceeding can be the indigent's most important avenue of access to justice with respect to problems of criminal prosecution, but who will represent the indigent in this proceeding? *Gideon* gives a right to counsel only for the criminal trial and appeal. The Supreme Court has held that there is no constitutional right to counsel in postconviction proceedings. In fact, the Court held that even an indigent prisoner on death row has no right to the assistance of counsel in bringing a postconviction claim involving constitutional defects at his capital trial. Some states provide appointed counsel for the postconviction claims of death row inmates, though usually the problems of low hourly rates and low maximum fees resurface in this context.

The upshot is that the uneducated, often illiterate indigent who needs to challenge the professional competence of his appointed counsel often must do so without professional help.

Thus, the indigent criminal defendant seeking access to justice faces monumental barriers in the form of low attorney fees, low caps, low aggregate expenditures, high-pressure assembly line representation, and inadequate remedies for ineffective assistance. . . .

Reform of the criminal justice process is a large task that requires attention to a variety of interrelated problems and a variety of forums for interrelated change. . . .

Modest steps could nonetheless radically improve the poor defendant's access to justice. Judicial standards for effective assistance could easily be given real content; postconviction remedies could be strengthened, especially by affording counsel for the indigent; and legislatures could mandate minimum standards of experience and effort for defense attorneys, especially in capital cases. Above all, meaningful reform requires more resources, adequately staffed defender organizations, and realistic compensation for appointed counsel.

These are remedies that benefit all of us. Proper restraint of prosecutorial power is the cornerstone of liberty in every free society. In the American justice system, the only reliable vehicle for ensuring that restraint is a vigorously functioning adversary system. As an Attorney General's Commission wrote almost thirty years ago, "The loss in vitality of the adversary system . . . significantly endangers the basic interests of a free community." Ultimately, access to justice for the underclass is our assurance of access to justice for all of us.

"Rehabilitation offers a constructive way to improve the criminal justice system. "

Focusing on Rehabilitation Would Improve the Criminal Justice System

Edgardo Rotman

In the following viewpoint, Edgardo Rotman states that the criminal justice system's emphasis on imprisonment does not promote justice. He believes that rehabilitation is a more just and effective way for society to control offenders and restore them to society. Rotman is an international law librarian at the University of Miami School of Law, in Coral Gables, Florida.

As you read, consider the following questions:

1. Why does Rotman believe that rehabilitation offers a better solution to the problems of the criminal justice system than longer prison sentences?
2. According to the author, why is imprisonment by itself ineffective in reducing crime?
3. How can the community effectively incorporate the rehabilitative method, according to Rotman?

Rehabilitation offers a constructive way to improve the criminal justice system. Its concern for offenders as whole human beings enriches the state's reaction to crime with a higher notion of justice and leads to a better law. Modern rehabilitative policies challenge the fantasy that the dark side of society can be forgotten and its deviants simply packed off to prisons. Without rehabilitative efforts before and after their discharge, offenders' grave social and individual problems will usually lead them to further crime. Rehabilitation thus increases the protection of those fundamental values guaranteed by criminal law. Moreover, rehabilitation improves the criminal justice system by connecting it to the public health, educational, and social welfare systems. Giving a social dimension to criminal justice, rehabilitation multiplies its resources and increases its quality and effectiveness.

The Rehabilitative Model

Most of the well-meant criticism of rehabilitation fails to distinguish its two basic forms: one authoritarian, aiming to force normative compliance and institutional adjustment, and another humanistic, offering noncoercive dialogue and opportunity. The latter form of rehabilitation respects moral choice and individual values, and enhances self-determination and responsibility. In addition, it seeks to reorganize the community to which the offender returns, including the workplace, school, and family.

The liberty-centered perspective leads to the conception of rehabilitation as an offender's right, the culmination of a continuum of rights guaranteeing the dignity of human beings confronted with criminal conviction. The right to rehabilitation is defined as the right to an opportunity to return to society with a better chance of being a useful citizen and of staying out of prison. This right requires not only education and therapy but also a nondestructive prison environment and, when possible, less restrictive alternatives to incarceration. The right to rehabilitation is consistent with the drive toward the full restoration of prisoners' civil and political rights of citizenship after release.

Rehabilitation has undergone deep transformations over time, reflecting changing anthropological conceptions and broader social ideology. These transformations can be represented by four successive historical models: penitentiary, therapeutic, social learning, and rights oriented. The penitentiary model is centered on the basic elements of work, discipline, and moral education. The therapeutic model—criticized for viewing the criminal offender as sick—adds the valuable element of care, in the sense of help and assistance. The social-learning approach inspired the most remarkable rehabilitative experiments of this century. The rights-oriented model includes the viewpoint of the offender, recognizing rehabilitation as a substantive right independent from utilitarian considerations and transient penal strategies.

A System in Disgrace

The criminal justice system in America is a disgrace to a civilized nation that prides itself on decency and the belief in the intrinsic worth of every individual.

The criminal justice system in America today is a complete failure. The financial waste incurred by local communities, cities, states, and the federal government is unbelievable. The crimes committed against those who are victimized by the system are intolerable.

The human waste caused by the warehousing of prisoners is unconscionable. The reverberation to our society is found in an increasing crime rate, due to the failure of the criminal justice system to adequately rehabilitate rather than show contempt for prisoners. This cause and effect relationship is totally ignored.

Donald P. Lay, address before the National Association of Pretrial Services Agencies, September 23, 1990.

Rehabilitation has not been a unitary phenomenon, and its development through the penitentiary, therapeutic, social-learning, and rights-oriented models has not been a straightforward process. Instead, we see a pattern of relative progress, in which later models mix with earlier ones. The renewal of rehabilitative policies will require a careful evaluation of what has been done in the past to distinguish relevant and redeeming efforts from flawed experiments.

It is imperative to distinguish valid criticism of rehabilitation from the many misdirected attacks that are really aimed at different phenomena, such as prisons or indeterminate sentencing. Viewed as the culmination of a continuum of offenders' rights, rehabilitation can no longer provide a pretext for discretionary abuse on the part of sentencing and correctional authorities. Quite the contrary, a right to rehabilitation reinforces the legal status of the sentenced offender and requires sentencing and correctional policies compatible with rehabilitative prison conditions. Because of its deep connection with the essence of criminal punishment, the right to rehabilitation has a paramount constitutional significance. Countries that have decided to combat crime at the highest civilized level have fully recognized rehabilitation as a constitutional mandate.

Rehabilitation should no longer be made a scapegoat to explain the increase of crime rates and various flaws in the criminal justice system. This type of criticism aims to replace constructive correctional experiments with harsh sentences. But the effectiveness of punishment does not depend on its harshness but rather on its certainty and proportionality—as both eighteenth-century reformers and modern behavioral scientists agree. Rehabilitation does not oppose the measure of deterrence inherent in criminal punishment. It strives only to maintain punishment within the limits of a preexisting law, counteracting its unwarranted consequences.

It is wrong to argue that sociological theories of crime discredit rehabilitation. Only a rigid deterministic view of society or the individual is incompatible with the idea of rehabilitation. In fact, a sense of the role of society in the genesis of crime should deepen the rehabilitative concept beyond a mere readjustment to a criminogenic society. Constructive sociological criticism should not only help to improve the quality of rehabilitative programs but complement them with social policies that reach the community itself, improving the linkages of programs with families, schools, and the world of work.

Rehabilitation Works

Many critics took a dim view of rehabilitative effectiveness during the 1970s, embodied in the popularized apothegm "nothing works." In the 1980s a new era of cautious optimism has begun. Rehabilitation has been reaffirmed, and many instances of success proclaimed. This shift reflects not only correctional improvement, but also a refinement of evaluative methods and the identification of some fundamental flaws in the "nothing works" arguments, which exaggerated programs' failures and overlooked valuable results.

In any case, it is a mistake to focus exclusively on the issue of effectiveness. To do so is to take a one-sided view of rehabilitation, seeing it exclusively from the perspective of society, as part of governmental planning and social policy. When rehabilitation is also regarded as a right of the offender, its value independent of its outcome becomes evident. Although the effectiveness of rehabilitation is of vital importance, its rationale transcends its utility.

What about "incorrigible" offenders? This designation more often reflects correctional flaws, including the lack of rehabilitative support, than individual propensities. An offender who seems incorrigible within a particular rehabilitative context may be amenable to other, untried treatment approaches. Moreover, recidivism should not automatically lead to a conclusion of incorrigibility or justify incapacitation or overly extended incarceration. The incapacitation of dangerous offenders should be justified in its own right, strictly respecting constitutional safeguards and statutory limitations.

Imprisonment can never be rehabilitative in itself. Historically, a mistaken belief in the prison's rehabilitative efficacy was used to justify protracted incarceration and the excessive resort to imprisonment as a criminal sanction. In reality, the very fact of imprisonment creates the need to rehabilitate the inmate from the prison's own desocializing influence. The social and psychological effects of freedom deprivation demand a strong compensatory rehabilitative action. To subject the inmate to the harmful effects of imprisonment without allowing any possibility to counteract them is additional and unlawful punishment. Without opportunities for rehabilitation, at the educational, labor, and therapeutic levels, the warehoused offender inevitably deteriorates.

Overhauling the System

Punishment is one thing, but our current incarceration policies are wasteful and should be changed. Present policies breed further crime, dehumanize individuals, and require gross expenditures of tax dollars needed for other purposes. With our nation facing both societal and fiscal crises of unrivaled proportions, we must move quickly and forcefully to overhaul the current system.

Donald P. Lay, address before the National Association of Pretrial Services Agencies, September 23, 1990.

Because penal servitude and hard labor have been abolished by law, imprisonment in a modern civilized society should consist only of the deprivation of liberty. To administer such legal punishment without unwarranted side effects requires a positive rehabilitative action. This effort cannot be reduced to a discrete set of programs but should create a rehabilitative environment, by reorganizing the correctional institution and linking it with the community through various forms of furloughs and prerelease programs. A supportive intrainstitutional atmosphere should be geared toward enhancing the future life prospects of the individual offender.

A basic principle of modern corrections, directly linked with the rehabilitative aim, should be to make the conditions of prison life resemble those outside the prison as much as possible. The social bonds of the inmates should be maintained and visitation encouraged. The notion of an "open prison" should be a cornerstone of rehabilitation-oriented correctional reform, especially in the last stages of a prison sentence. The open prison should be oriented toward freedom and should support the inmate at the levels of education, work, and social welfare. The rehabilitative potential of prison work depends on its being integrated with the free labor market. Prison work should be meaningful, useful, productive, and realistic and should meet the requirements of the market.

Creating Alternatives

Efforts to avoid the pernicious effects of incarceration find their ultimate expression in the creation of noncustodial alternatives to incarceration. At the sentencing level, the rehabilitative aim should lead to the use of alternatives to imprisonment whenever possible. Short prison sentences should be replaced by nonincarcerative alternatives, and excessively long sentences should be minimized to avoid destructive effects on inmates and their chances of future social reintegration.

The most effective way to carry out the rehabilitative task is to deal with offenders in the community. Genuine community corrections actually replace imprisonment and can never be used to extend state intervention beyond its indispensable minimum. The community should not be considered a panacea in itself. The value of a concrete community for corrections depends on its cohesion, educational and moral resources, and its low criminogenic potential. As ideal conditions seldom prevail, a modern rehabilitative concept should be supplemented with action on the community to reorganize and transform it into an opportunity-providing social context.

A right to rehabilitation includes a right to be considered for probation, community service, or other available community-based programs. These rights should be exercised according to objective guidelines ensuring fair treatment. Probation—a fruitful field for improvement and creative innovation—should remain a centerpiece of a modern rehabilitative policy. Suspended sentences, which rely on offenders' responsibility and conscience, should be maintained as a way to impel them to assume themselves the task of integration into the community. Other nonincarcerative sanctions, such as fines, should also be used.

Traditional alternatives to imprisonment have been supplemented by community service sentences and restitution, which have achieved remarkable rehabilitative success, by creating a positive interaction with the community. Rehabilitation in the community, through various types of support centers, can be an alternative not only to arrest and pretrial detention, but also to prosecution. Mediation and arbitration of minor criminal cases by community representatives have become fruitful alternatives to adjudication in the courts, representing an important form of social learning and a powerful factor for attitude change.

"Between crime and punishment lies the criminal-justice system, and Americans must be aware that theirs is breaking down."

The Adversary System Should Be Replaced

Charles Maechling Jr.

In the following viewpoint, Charles Maechling Jr. states that the criminal justice system is outdated and needs reform. The present system is based on an adversary philosophy where lawyers battle one another in court to establish the guilt or innocence of criminal defendants. Maechling argues that the system is bogged down with procedures that allow abuses in criminal trials. In addition, he contends that lawyers are only concerned with winning and not with finding the guilt or innocence of a defendant. Maechling, a guest scholar at the Brookings Institution in Washington, D.C., is a former professor of law at the University of Virginia in Petersburg and a former member of the law faculty of Cambridge University in England.

As you read, consider the following questions:

1. What is the purpose of the American criminal justice system, according to Maechling?
2. According to the author, why is the European civil law system better than the system used in the United States?
3. What proposals does Maechling suggest American criminal courts should borrow from European civil law?

Charles Maechling Jr., "Borrowing from Europe's Civil Law Tradition," *ABA Journal* 77 (January 1991): 59-63. Copyright © 1991 by the American Bar Association. Reprinted by permission of the *ABA Journal*.

Between crime and punishment lies the criminal-justice system, and Americans must be aware that theirs is breaking down. Court calendars and prisons are clogged. It can take years to execute a child murderer or put a rapist behind bars, while an otherwise harmless teenager can get a mandatory 20-year sentence for mere possession of cocaine. One Southern state sentenced an ignorant black youth to five years at hard labor for shoplifting a $6 item.

The simultaneous harshness and ineffectiveness of the American system stems in part from a major and little-explored root—the adversarial nature of our courts. All European countries except Great Britain and Ireland, and nearly all Third World countries with a European cultural heritage, employ variations of the so-called inquisitorial method, which is rooted in the 2,000-year tradition of the civil or Roman law.

An Inadequate System

Only the Anglo-Saxon countries cling to a judicial parody of the medieval tournament—lawyers for the state and the defense fight for the body of the accused before a judge as umpire and a jury carefully selected for its ignorance of the personalities and issues before it.

The narrow focus on the accused, coupled with the disproportionate power and authority of the state, necessitates a bristling array of constitutional safeguards and procedural rules to level the jousting field and protect the defendant's rights. The tournament, or trial, is the supreme event: Nothing in the prior stages of the criminal justice process has any validity until proved to the satisfaction of the jury in open court.

Anglo-American trial procedure has a limited purpose—to enforce the tournament rules. As every first-year law student learns, the function of the trial is not to establish the truth: It is to provide the prosecution with a forum to convince the jury beyond a reasonable doubt that the accused is guilty of the specific crime he is charged with, and nothing else.

The process requires the prosecution to present its case in the most awkward way possible—through a succession of witnesses, each of whom lifts the curtain on a separate aspect of the events in question. Each witness is held to the confines of his own personal experience, and the last thing a witness is allowed to do is tell his story in his own words and give his opinion of what it means.

Moreover, to lend credibility to his testimony and avoid having it discredited on cross-examination he must profess absolute certainty about what he saw or heard. This leaves the veracity of trial testimony always open to question. The police record of statements made by witnesses at the time has no probative value of its own, and the average person cannot, without coaching or prompting, remember the details of events that he witnessed the week before, let alone six months or a year ago.

Another distortion is imposed by the hearsay rule. In the adversarial process the jury is not allowed to hear what the witness says another person told him he heard or saw at the time. The only exception in Britain, Canada, and some other jurisdictions is what the accused told the witness or may have said in the latter's presence. This wipes out a whole area of valuable information that is especially useful in the prosecution of conspiracies, racketeering and white-collar crimes.

"Your honour, we find the defendant guilty, the court room jammed, the docket overloaded, the calendar crowded, the jails full, the system appalling, but what can you do?"

An artificial obstacle now more or less unique to the United States is the exclusion of illegally seized evidence. No reasonable person would question that the Fourth Amendment prohibition against unreasonable searches and seizures is an essential freedom of a democratic society. But why it should be allowed to interfere with criminal prosecutions and, under the "fruit of the poisonous tree" doctrine, bar legally obtained evidence as well, defies common sense. . . .

The adversarial system is at its worst in the ritual of cross-examination. The witness who tries to give a frank and honest statement of his observations, impressions and beliefs, with all the necessary qualifications, will find his recollection challenged at every step. In most cases he will be forced to retract or to re-state only those portions that he can testify to with precision and absolute certainty. Ostensibly designed to narrow testimony down to a hard core of "fact," cross-examination more often confuses the witness and muddies the record. This is exactly what the cross-examiner intends. His object is to seize on contradictions and uncertainties in order to discredit the witness. . . .

Flawed Procedures

Deprived of a great deal of relevant information, and forced by the rules to receive what is deemed admissible in piecemeal form removed from real-life context, the jury is required to determine guilt or innocence on the narrowest grounds possible.

The choice is not "what, if anything, did the defendant do that was against the law?" but "did the defendant do exactly what the prosecution alleges?" Unless specified in the indictment, there is no possibility, for example, of convicting an accused of arson as well as burglary, no matter how overwhelming the evidence that emerges at trial that he set fire to the house he burgled.

The mock tournament aspects of the accusatorial process are also prejudicial to the accused. Since the prosecution needs to build a bulletproof case beyond reasonable doubt, it tends to accumulate only information that reinforces the initial presumption of a suspect's guilt, and to disregard or discount information that contradicts or qualifies it. The need to establish criminal intent also puts a premium on over-certainty, pseudo-precision and one-dimensional interpretation of the evidence.

Two other abuses that spring from the accusatorial process are the plea bargain and the temptation to fabricate evidence. The plea bargain does little damage to the integrity of the system as long as it is limited to one individual; it has the practical benefit of saving the state from the expense and effort of time-consuming trials and appeals, and from overloading the system.

But once transformed into an instrument for convicting conspirators and co-defendants, it opens the door to dishonesty and gross injustice. A criminal defendant who breaks with his confederates and succumbs to the lure of a light sentence or no sentence at all is likely to give the prosecution everything it wants—testimony to incriminate others, embellished with all requisite certainty.

Worse, plea bargains are increasingly made with the defendant in the best position to implicate others—not with a minor accomplice to nail the ringleader. In the Walker espionage case, for example, the mastermind of the ring was allowed to plea-bargain his way to a light sentence, while his hapless brother-in-law, pressed into service virtually against his will, received a sadistic 25-year sentence without parole for turning over one low-grade security item.

Civil law countries reject the plea-bargain practice as tainted and make it a bar to extradition.

The civil law tradition that governs the countries of western Europe, which has been retained in Eastern Europe as well, proceeds from premises so different from the Anglo-Saxon tradition that it can easily delude Americans into imagining the worst.

For starters, the name "inquisitorial" applied to a criminal justice process conjures up "inquisition" rather than the actual derivation from "inquiry." The notion that justice can be served by objective methods of inquiry rather than by pit-bull confrontations in a judicial arena leaves the average American uneasy about his ability to fight back. This is especially true if he assumes that in Europe the accused is presumed guilty until proved innocent.

The inquisitorial process does not make the trial the supreme event in the way the accusatorial process does: It is rather the public finale of an ongoing investigation.

In a felony case the process breaks down into three stages—an initial investigatory phase conducted by the police; an examining phase, conducted by an examining magistrate (in France, the *juge d'instruction*); and the trial, conducted by the state prosecutor before a small panel of judges, supplemented in some countries by lay judges or a small jury. The examining phase is both a more detailed investigation and a preliminary in camera trial to determine whether the case against a suspect is strong enough to bring him before a more formal tribunal.

The function of the magistrate in the examining phase is the development and assessment of all the information surrounding a crime. This encompasses not only what is produced by the police during the investigative phase but what is subsequently extracted by the examining magistrate from the witnesses, physical evidence and information provided from other sources.

Civil Law Procedures

In the civil law system, the dossier, or official record, plays a crucial role. Every relevant scrap of information about the case and the individuals involved in it goes into the dossier; nothing relevant is excluded. The task of the examining magistrate is to sift through this material, weigh it for what it is worth, and make a judgment as to whether it adds up to a prima facie case.

Well into the examining phase, the focus is likely to be on the event rather than on a particular suspect. Thereafter, the emphasis is on building a coherent case based on all the information available. This involves accumulation of corroborative evidence pointing to one conclusion, but always leaving that conclusion open to challenge by new evidence and contradictory testimony. . . .

At the trial, the public prosecutor will present the case against the accused by in effect distilling the dossier into coherent form, not in rehashing its content through the testimony of one witness after another. Witnesses may, however, be requested by the defense to refute the information in the dossier or by the court to resolve crucial questions or apparent anomalies. The court does the questioning, although the lawyers may cross-examine. All witnesses are the court's witnesses, though either side may propose them. . . .

Questionable Partnerships

The fact of the matter is that the Constitution is no longer the backbone of our judicial system—circumventing it has become the backbone. . . .

To circumvent the Constitution, the adversary system of justice on which our entire criminal justice system is based has been undermined by the symbiotic relationship between judges, prosecutors, and defense lawyers—especially state-paid and state-monitored public defenders.

Jan Harlan Kristian, *The Prison Mirror*, August 12, 1988.

In civil law jurisdictions, the rights of suspects and defendants are safeguarded, but not in the same way as here or in other Anglo-Saxon countries. In the civil law world the process itself provides safeguards. As noted, the focus is initially on the event, not the person—first, to determine whether a crime took place and only thereafter to zero in on a particular suspect. The accused has the right to counsel almost from the moment of his arrest and can refuse to answer questions. However, a negative inference may be drawn from his refusal to answer and anything he does say may be used against him.

The admissibility of all evidence for what it is worth can also work in his favor: background information that in an adversarial proceeding would be ruled irrelevant until sentencing can be introduced at any stage to show mitigating circumstances. Judicial rulings and sentencing will be the product of the collective judgment of a judicial panel and not dependent on the arbitrary judgment of a single, all-powerful judge. . . .

Furthermore, paperwork is kept to a minimum: Objections and motions are rarely reduced to writing and almost never appealed; if there is a dispute over a point of law, the law books are handed up to the judge, who makes a ruling on the spot. The sentence usually follows immediately after the verdict. The trial transcript is generally considered sufficient for an appeal, which is processed in 90 days or less and, except in unusual circumstance, is confined to review of the evidence.

Reinterpreting the Law

Whether the deficiencies of the American adversarial method can be rectified is an open question. Indeed, at first glance, the U.S. Constitution and Bill of Rights do appear to raise insuperable barriers to change.

But closer examination will reveal that many of the anachronisms discussed above are not anchored in the specific language of the Constitution. They are either the product of later interpretation by the Supreme Court or derive from British precedents that, in turn, trace their origins to medieval abuses and the long struggle for power between Parliament and the Crown.

For example:

• There is nothing in the Bill of Rights that requires that evidence procured in violation of the Fourth Amendment prohibition against unreasonable searches and seizures be inadmissible in court. To the contrary, the early history of this provision indicates that it was designed to protect private property and the integrity of the home—to stand on its own feet with its own penalties, rather than to interfere with the prosecution of criminals. The exclusionary rule in federal courts dates back only to 1914, and in state courts to the 1961 decision in *Mapp v. Ohio*, 367 U.S. 643. In 1949, Justice Felix Frankfurter invited Congress to overturn the rule. *Wolf v. Colorado*, 338 U.S. 25.

• The Fifth Amendment prohibition against self-incrimination could be restored by the Supreme Court to its declared purpose of preventing self-incrimination in a criminal case against the accused, and removed as an excuse for allowing a defendant to evade truthful responses in congressional inquiries and other forums.

The archaic rule against admission of hearsay evidence—the kind of information governments and ordinary people use daily to make decisions—finds no mention in the Constitution and could be eliminated at a stroke by legislative fiat.

• There is no reason to disqualify the best educated and better informed citizenry from jury duty simply because they have acquired general knowledge of a crime or personality from the news media, as in the Iran-contra trials. The Sixth Amendment requirement of impartiality need not be a mandate for political illiteracy.

• There is also no reason why all witnesses in a criminal trial—especially "expert" witnesses picked for their biases and coached to give slanted testimony—should not be witnesses for the court, selected and screened for competence and objectivity. Or why most of the questioning of witnesses should not be the function of the judge, with the lawyers only permitted a limited right of final questioning.

• Finally, there is nothing in the Constitution to prevent limiting criminal appeals to one appeal confined to review of the evidence, absent a showing of some gross irregularity at the trial. Legislation or judicial ruling could accomplish these and other improvements drawn from the civil law tradition without starting down the futile road of trying to amend the Constitution.

In the United States, the criminal justice process is now politicized in a way unknown in other civilized countries. Courts have become arenas of ideological conflict in which the overriding questions of guilt or innocence are eclipsed by disputes about constitutional safeguards.

If fairness is the issue, one should note the words of Professor John Merryman of Stanford, a leading comparative-law scholar: "If innocent, he would prefer to be tried by a civil law court; but if he were guilty, he would prefer to be tried by a common law court." This country may be unable to embrace all parts of the civil law tradition, but it should at least consider borrowing from it.

> *"Victims and offenders often become frustrated and angry as they move through the criminal justice system."*

Establish Mediation Between Victims and Offenders

Mark S. Umbreit

In the following two-part viewpoint, Mark S. Umbreit contends that the criminal justice system would be more just if it allowed victims to confront those who have harmed them. In addition, Umbreit argues that mediation between victims and offenders would give offenders a chance to apologize for the harm they have caused. Umbreit is the director of research and training at the Center for Victim Offender Mediation, an assistant professor in the School of Social Work at the University of Minnesota, both in Minneapolis, and author of the book *Crime and Reconciliation*.

As you read, consider the following questions:

1. Why is the criminal justice system's focus on punishment inadequate for crime victims, according to Umbreit?
2. Why does the author emphasize that both the victim and offender must voluntarily decide to mediate their differences?
3. What three things did the victims of crime like most about the mediation program, according to Umbreit?

Mark S. Umbreit, "Having Offenders Meet with Their Victims Offers Benefits for Both Parties," *Corrections Today*, July 1991 and "Minnesota Mediation Center Produces Positive Results," *Corrections Today*, August 1991, vol. 53, no. 5. Reprinted with permission of the American Correctional Association.

I

Crime victims frequently feel powerless and vulnerable. Some feel twice victimized—first by the offender and then by a justice system that often doesn't address their needs. Offenders, meanwhile, rarely understand or are confronted with the human dimension of their criminal behavior—that victims are real people, not faceless objects without feelings. It's not surprising, then, that victims and offenders often become frustrated and angry as they move through the criminal justice system.

The principles of "retributive justice" tend to dominate our nation's response to crime and victimization. The criminal justice system focuses on the State as the victim, with the individual victim placed in a very passive role. Adversarial relationships are considered normal, and offenders are generally punished severely to deter future crime. The personal character of criminal behavior is given little attention.

A Different View of Justice

A new vision of justice, however, is attracting growing national interest. "Restorative justice" emphasizes that crime is a violation of one person by another, rather than simply against the State. Dialogue and negotiation are central to restorative justice, and problem solving for the future is seen as more important than establishing blame for past behavior.

Severe offender punishment is less important than empowering victims in their search for closure, impressing on offenders the real human impact of their behavior and promoting restitution to victims. Instead of ignoring victims and placing offenders in a passive role, restorative justice places offenders and their victims together in problem-solving roles.

Restorative justice principles are now used in a growing number of communities throughout North America and Europe. Crime victims are meeting with their offenders, talking about the crime, expressing their concerns and negotiating restitution. With roots dating to the early 1970s in the Midwest, victim/offender mediation and reconciliation programs now exist in more than 100 jurisdictions in the United States, 54 in Norway, 40 in France, 25 in Canada, 25 in Germany, 18 in England, 20 in Finland and eight in Belgium.

Most programs are sponsored by private organizations working closely with the courts. But more probation departments and other public agencies, including the Oklahoma Department of Corrections, are becoming sponsors of their own victim/offender mediation programs.

The mediation process begins when offenders—most often those convicted of non-violent property offenses—are referred by the court. Some programs work with juvenile or adult offenders who are diverted from further court processing if the mediation is successful. A small number of programs are beginning to work with more serious violent crimes and are reporting good results, although a more intense case management and mediation process is required.

Victims Meeting Offenders

Each case is assigned to either a staff or volunteer mediator, who meets with the offender and victim separately before the mediation session is scheduled. During these individual sessions, the mediator listens to each party's story, explains the program and encourages their participation. This encouragement is by no means coercive; the process is meant to empower victims and offenders by presenting them with choices.

If both parties are willing, the mediator schedules a face-to-face meeting. The meeting begins with the mediator explaining his or her role, identifying the agenda and stating any ground rules that may be necessary, such as allowing each party to complete their statements before interrupting them with questions or comments.

High Rate of Satisfaction

Victim-offender mediation projects have uniformly resulted in (1) extremely high levels of victim satisfaction in terms of the perceived fairness of the processes as well as the outcome of negotiations with offenders; (2) at least modest reduction in offender recidivism; and (3) higher levels of actual compensation received by victims than through the formal criminal justice process or other victim restitution programs.

Victims consistently report their appreciation for having the opportunity to tell their stories and to confront offenders with their sense of injury, anger and outrage. Responses by offenders show more frequent acknowledgement of guilt, deeper appreciation for the consequences of their wrongdoing and a greater sense of remorse.

John O. Haley, *Crime and Justice Network Newsletter*, July/August/September 1991.

The first part of the meeting focuses on a discussion of the facts and feelings related to the crime. Victims are given the opportunity to express their feelings directly to the person who violated them, as well as to receive answers to lingering questions such as "Why me?" or "Were you stalking us and planning on coming back?"

While offenders are put in the uncomfortable position of having to face the people they violated, they also are given the rare chance to show a more human dimension to their characters and to express remorse in a very personal way.

In the second part of the meeting, the participants discuss what the victim "lost" and work out a mutually acceptable restitution agreement. This offers a tangible symbol of conflict resolution and a focal point for accountability. Mediators do not impose the restitution settlement.

Effective Criminal Justice Tool

In more than 95 percent of meetings in many programs, a written restitution agreement is negotiated and signed at the end of the meeting by the victim, the offender and the mediator. When agreements cannot be reached, the case is returned to the court for determination of restitution.

The mediation process helps victims reduce their anger, frustration and fear and compensates them for their losses. Offenders, meanwhile, are held accountable for their behavior and have the chance to make amends. Some are even diverted from initial or continued costly incarceration in jails or prisons.

Evaluations of programs in Minnesota and Indiana have found that both victims and offenders benefit from this humanizing experience with the justice system. The vast majority of participants express satisfaction with the meetings and indicate the process and outcome were fair. Although it is not appropriate in all cases, victim/offender mediation is an effective criminal justice tool that vividly expresses the principles of restorative justice.

II

More and more communities in the United States, Canada and Europe are offering crime victims the chance to meet their offenders, discuss the crime, express their concerns and negotiate mutually agreeable restitution plans. Working closely with local courts and probation departments, these victim/offender mediation and reconciliation programs are making an important contribution to meeting the needs of many crime victims, offenders and court systems.

A Case Study

One such program is the Center for Victim Offender Mediation, or CVOM, in Minneapolis, Minn. CVOM, which began in 1985, is a program of the Minnesota Citizens Council on Crime and Justice, a private non-profit agency operating several programs for crime victims, offenders and their families. It receives referrals of juvenile offenders from court services staff in Hennepin and Ramsey counties, which include Minneapolis and St. Paul.

46

Participation in the mediation process is voluntary for victims and offenders. Once a case is referred by the court, it is assigned to a staff or volunteer mediator. The mediator first meets with the offender and victim separately to hear their stories, explain the program and encourage participation. If both are willing, a mediation session is scheduled.

In 1989, I began analyzing the CVOM's effectiveness. My study was based on post-mediation interviews with a sample of 51 victims and 66 juvenile offenders.

A total of 379 cases were referred to the CVOM in 1989, representing 228 individual victims and 257 individual offenders; some crimes had multiple victims and/or offenders.

Healing Victims and Offenders

At Victim-Offender Reconciliation Group we hold the view that the offender—not society—is responsible for his offense and that crime is a moral habit created entirely by personal choice. The only prerequisite for membership in the program is that the offender be able to freely admit his complete culpability for his crime. This is key. Crime is not a sociological aberration, it is sin. Crime comes from the human heart, and it is there that real reform must take place. Reform cannot be mandated by the state, and membership in the program is voluntary on the part of the inmate. The VORG program has more inmate applicants than room in the program for them. What we have discovered is that there are many victims and many offenders who desire reconciliation and resolution, and we only provide a format for this healing to occur.

Januarius E. Rodrigues, *Crime and Justice Network Newsletter*, July/August/September 1991.

Fifty-six percent of these referrals were misdemeanor offenses and 44 percent were felony offenses. The most common offenses were vandalism (32 percent), theft (25 percent), burglary (15 percent) and tampering (11 percent). Other offenses included car theft (8 percent), assault (6 percent) and robbery (3 percent). Sixty-one percent of the referrals occurred after adjudication and 39 percent occurred as a diversion from adjudication. Following are some key findings:

• Of the 379 cases, 50 percent resulted in face-to-face mediation, 9 percent in indirect mediation and 41 percent in no mediation. The latter cases were returned to the court.

• Restitution agreements were reached in 96 percent of the mediation cases. These agreements resulted in a total of $23,328 in monetary restitution, 403 hours of personal service restitution for the victim, 787 hours of community service restitution and 17 agreements with only an apology required by the victim.

• Eighty-one percent of restitution agreements were successfully completed.

Victims' Impressions

A number of reasons were offered for those cases that did not enter the mediation process: the victim was unwilling (36 percent); the offender was unwilling (24 percent); the conflict was resolved by the parties prior to the court referral (17 percent); and one of the parties could not be located.

Both crime victims and their offenders indicated a high level of satisfaction with the mediation process. Consistent with prior research, victims who met with their offenders in the CVOM program indicated that being able to meet the offender, talk about what happened, express their concerns and work out a restitution plan was more important than actually receiving compensation for their losses.

While 76 percent of victims stated that receiving restitution was important, 92 percent indicated other, more important non-monetary benefits, such as getting answers and telling their offender how the crime affected them. Also consistent with prior research, 88 percent of victims were concerned about offenders' needs for counseling and other rehabilitative services.

Three themes emerged regarding what crime victims liked most about mediation. First, telling the offender how the crime affected them emotionally and/or financially was important. "It was a chance to tell the offender the hardship it put on us as a family," one victim said.

The importance of being able to directly confront the offender was the second theme. "I liked that the kid had to look me in the eyes," said another.

Helping the person who victimized them was the third most common theme expressed by victims. Said one victim, "I wanted most of all to help the boy."

Overall Positive Response

Crime victims had positive attitudes regarding the actual mediation session and its outcome. Ninety percent felt good about being in the mediation program, and nearly all felt the restitution agreement was fair to both parties. Eighty-six percent of victims said meeting their offender was helpful, and the majority—55 percent—had a positive attitude toward their offender. Following the mediation, 94 percent of victims experienced no fear of re-victimization by their offender.

Victims who participated in mediation were overwhelmingly satisfied with the program. The only things several victims said they disliked about the mediation program were their anxiety before the meeting and their initial tension in the mediation session. Some made comments such as "I felt nervous" and "It was a very tense situation."

Juvenile offenders were also satisfied with the program. Telling the victim what happened, working out a mutually acceptable restitution plan, paying back the victim and apologizing to the victim were important issues to 90 percent of offenders. Ninety-five percent apologized to their victims.

Innovative Resolutions

Victim-offender reconciliation programs (VORPs) and mediation programs . . . bring together, with the consent of all parties, the victim and the offender for face-to-face meetings. Once a meeting is agreed to, which happens in about half of the cases referred to VORPs, most encounters end in agreement, usually a signed contract that involves restitution. While most VORPs deal with property crimes, programs in Winnipeg, Manitoba, and in Genessee County, New York have successfully mediated manslaughter and rape cases.

Bill Douglas, *Christianity and Crisis*, May 13, 1991.

Eighty-eight percent of offenders said the restitution agreements were fair to them and 95 percent indicated they were fair to their victims. Ninety-four percent felt it was helpful to meet their victims, 95 percent were feeling better after meeting their victims, 84 percent believed their victims had a better opinion of them and nearly all—96 percent—would suggest victim/offender mediation to a friend.

Overall, offenders indicated slightly less satisfaction with mediation than did their victims. Whereas 92 percent of victims indicated a positive attitude toward their mediator, 88 percent of offenders did.

Several themes emerged in response to questions about what offenders liked most and least about the mediation program. Getting to know the victim, finding out the victim was nice and that the victim understood them were the most common themes expressed by the juvenile offenders in this study. "He understood the mistake I made, and I really did appreciate him for it," one youth said.

The quality of the communication between offenders and victims was also a common theme. "I liked that we could talk and get things out in the open," said another.

Like their victims, the most common thing offenders disliked

49

was the anxiety they experienced before and during the meeting. Comments included, "It was hard meeting him face to face," "It was kind of scary and nerve-wracking" and "I felt kind of stupid and guilty because he was real sad, but it felt better after I had a chance to apologize."

The results of this research cannot be generalized beyond the CVOM. Far more research is required to more thoroughly examine the victim/offender mediation process in multiple sites using matched comparison group samples that were not referred to the mediation program. This study is consistent, however, with a small but growing body of research that has found mediation to be an effective way to resolve conflict between some crime victims and their offenders.

"The present system of criminal justice is not working, and never really has."

A Variety of Measures Are Needed to Improve the System

Daryl F. Gates

Daryl F. Gates is the former police chief of the Los Angeles Police Department (LAPD). During his twenty years as police chief, Gates was a controversial figure. While many citizens perceived him as effective at bringing law and order to the city, many others blamed him for causing divisions and for doing nothing to stop police brutality. In the following viewpoint, Gates argues that the present criminal justice system is ineffective and offers several suggestions on how to improve it.

As you read, consider the following questions:

1. Why does Gates say that more police will not solve the crime problem?
2. What is the attitude of most people who are asked to get involved with community policing, according to the author?
3. What does Gates mean when he says that the police must provide "quality service"?

We have become an oppressed nation. We willingly trip off to war, depleting our material resources and sacrificing our young, to free other people who are living under oppression. Yet we continue to allow ourselves to be oppressed by the presence of a criminal army, which sucks up more and more of our freedom. Our answer: More police!

Which is idiotic. More money, more police, more courts, more jails—these are solutions that make no sense. Already the citizens of Los Angeles spend $1 billion a year on police protection; they are being soaked enough. This is not a police state; it's supposed to be a democracy. Do we want to go about our lives with still *more* cops looking over our shoulders? In America, the land of the free?

Improving the Criminal Justice System

The present system of criminal justice is not working, and never really has. I've thought long, often, and hard about how the system can be improved. Here are some of my ideas:

1. *Identify the Enemy.* . . .We know that in the United States, 2.7 million adults were on formal probation and 531,000 were on parole in 1991. Add to these figures the number of adults in prison or in jail, and the total number of adults under correctional supervision was 3.7 million. On any given day then, 1 out of 49 adults was under some form of correctional supervision. That breaks down to 1 out of every 27 men, and 1 out of every 194 women. Throw in another million or more who have not been caught or who are awaiting trial.

Using this kind of data within each state and city, carefully organized by the types of crimes most likely to be committed, each police agency could begin to determine the dimensions of the criminal army it faces.

When I first came on the force in 1949 we arrested 110,000 drunks a year. It sounded like a huge number—my God, was everyone in Los Angeles tipsy? One day a sergeant said, "How come we have to fingerprint these drunks each time they're brought in? I mean, they bring old Joe in every other week."

It suddenly dawned on us that maybe we didn't have 110,000 drunks after all. Using old IBM punch cards, we were able to organize what we called our "drunk repeater file." When Joe would be brought in, we would look up his card and just add another thumbprint.

It turned out we had 22,000 or 23,000 people arrested on intoxication charges, not 110,000. . . .

Preventing Crime

2. *End Parole and Probation.* They're useless. Both ostensibly provide control over a convicted person while providing direc-

tion toward noncriminal behavior. It sounds good, but it doesn't work and never has. A study by the Rand Corporation determined that within two years' time, two thirds of those released on probation commit crimes that lead to their rearrest. Studies made in the 1950s produced similar results. Some progress.

Parole has the same failure. A bill signed into law by former Governor Jerry Brown limits parole in California to one year. Others convicted of crimes never serve any time and are sentenced to probation. Los Angeles County spends $300 million a year on probation and boasts some of the finest people in the field anywhere. But with an average caseload of four hundred offenders, how much control can one probation officer exert? It is impossible for one caseworker to keep tabs on the whereabouts, weekly, of four hundred probationers. Many disappear—until they are arrested again. Parole officers are saddled with the same unreasonable caseloads and aren't effective either.

Knowing the Enemy

To fight a war on crime, shouldn't we at least know the size of the criminal army? When General Norman Schwarzkopf marched into Kuwait, he knew the exact dimensions of the enemy and the firepower it possessed. In America no attempt has ever been made to measure the number of burglars, robbers, murderers, or rapists. We diligently count crimes and arrests, but we pay scant attention to determining the number of criminals who perpetrate these crimes. Ask any police chief in the country to estimate the number of people he believes are committing burglaries, robberies, car thefts, and so on, in his community and he'll give you a wild guess. With a little study, and some help from all of our computerized systems, law enforcement has the ability to make some fairly accurate assessments.

Daryl F. Gates, *Chief: My Life in the LAPD*, 1992.

Instead of these useless tactics, I have long advocated doing away with parole and probation altogether. Rather, depending upon the severity of the crime, how dangerous the person is, and his or her personal history, a judge would sentence the convicted person to "in-prison" or "out-prison" status.

This is a complex proposal, but in a nutshell this is how it would work: In-prisoners would go straight to prison to do their time, while those who would now be likely to be placed on probation would be given out-prison status. They would be sentenced to their homes and controlled by strict conditions of outprison status. . . .

3. *Crime Prevention Starts with Kids.* The front end of the system means the children. We are simply not doing enough to prevent so many of our young people from becoming criminals.

If all the talented parole and probation workers could be freed from their ineffectual supervision of criminals and reassigned to working with potentially endangered children, it would be like mining a bright, shiny vein of gold. Programs could be designed to work with children who come from unstable home environments or live in troubled neighborhoods. We could redirect vast resources from the tail end of the system to the front end. We could reach children before they became criminals, not afterwards. It would be a massive effort to stem the flow of new recruits into that criminal army. . . .

Communities and Police

4. *Community-Oriented Policing.* As law enforcement limps along, this is the hot idea of the moment sweeping police literature. Started in nineteenth-century London by Sir Robert Peel, community-oriented policing was nothing more than bobbies walking a beat. The concept is used effectively in Japan, where *Kobans,* or guard shacks, now exist in every neighborhood. Inside sits the local police officer. People know they can go to that officer with a problem. Tokyo has thousands of *Kobans,* and the system has made the Japanese feel comfortable moving about their cities.

As this plan of forging an alliance between officers and the neighborhoods they serve spreads across America, the first problem is the need for more officers. Commissioner Lee Brown of the New York Police Department is a strong supporter of community-based policing. Already he has a department pushing 28,000 officers, in addition to the city's transit police, harbor police, housing authority police, and airport police. Now Lee is asking for 6,000 additional officers to put into neighborhoods. But again, how much more can taxpayers be asked to pay for?

Officers are only half of the partnership that needs to be formed. For this concept to work, the neighborhood must be actively involved, and many people don't want to bother. They want to come home at night, know they can rest safely, walk the streets after dark, and maybe say a friendly hello to the officer—but that's all the interaction with the police they want. Their attitude is: It's *their* job to stop crime—let *them* do it. . . .

The problem is that too many people mistake community-oriented policing as a cure-all for crime. It is not. There is anecdotal evidence that it makes people feel better about the police, and the police, in turn, feel better about the people. It does bring the police and the community closer together—but that doesn't mean we're providing better service.

5. *Quality of Service.* A police department puts out a product, just as a company does. Our product is a service: to maintain peace and to reduce crime and violence so that people feel safe. Like that of any company in the private sector, our goal should be customer satisfaction. This is an area of law enforcement—indeed of government—that is routinely overlooked. Community-based policing is fine, but it doesn't go far enough toward satisfying our customers. Rarely do we even bother to find out what the customer wants. That's bad business. . . .

Controlling Criminal Leaks

With jails and prisons overflowing, those convicted rarely serve out their sentences. In California, state prisons release 20,000 of their inmates within three months; 40,000 are released after six months; and 60,000 in less than a year. Then they recirculate. In 1989, for instance, 11,040 parolees were returned to prison. The way the system is designed, the police, the courts, and the jails just keep coming in to perform the same job over and over. If you had a leaky pipe, you wouldn't keep calling a plumber to patch it up—you'd get a new pipe. It would be fixed, and the leak controlled.

We need to begin to control our criminal leaks, too, putting an end to the faulty patchwork.

Daryl F. Gates, *Chief: My Life in the LAPD,* 1992.

The public's perception of what needs to be done is often at odds with that of the police. People will complain about a panhandler begging in front of a store. They will raise Cain about drunks on a street corner where their kids must cross on the way to school, or about men who loiter outside a laundromat making jokes when women walk by. It is likely that none of these people actually present a threat, but the public feels intimidated nonetheless.

Graffiti on a subway car or bus makes passengers feel no one is in control. They may not be in any danger, but they feel as if they are. James Q. Wilson and George Kelling, in their paper "Broken Windows," speak eloquently to this phenomenon of public-disorder concerns. Perceptions of danger are often magnified by the media. In living color, a drive-by shooting in Los Angeles will come right into your living room; then there will be big headlines to suffer as you drink your morning coffee. The city can panic over too much, and too explicit, media coverage. Even though the chances of someone's dying in such a manner are remote, there comes the cry: "Where are the police? We need more police!"

Adjusting and melding the public's priorities with those of the police is a chief's job. I found, for instance, that pulling a drunk, who isn't going to hurt anybody, off a street corner does more for neighborhood psychology than putting away a burglar who, operating two blocks away, does real harm. Only the victims are aware of the burglar; *everyone* sees the drunk. Quality service requires that the police attend to both: Satisfy the concern over the drunk, but go after the burglar to assure safety to the community that is unaware of the danger. That is quality service. . . .

Less Political Control

6. *Free the Chief.* It would be difficult for a Corporate Executive Officer to run a company if he had to produce a quality product, yet had no control over the size of his budget or how it was allocated. Such is my plight, as well as that of most of the police chiefs in the nation.

Clearly, the amount of money allocated to policing is a policy decision that must be made by politicians. But the lack of control by the chief of police after that decision is made is appalling. I've often said to the political leadership: "Just tell me how much you are willing to spend on the police department and then give me some flexibility in how that money is spent." But that isn't the way it works. . . .

Chiefs could use a little independence from political control. They should be held accountable, of course, but the manipulation of chiefs and police departments by political leadership has become excessive and has long been the stuff that corruption is made of. One of the reasons the director of the Federal Bureau of Investigation has been given a ten-year term is to avoid the attempts at political manipulation that occurred during Richard Nixon's time. While I'm not advocating a total lack of political or civilian control of the police chief, I am simply speaking of that ounce of independence that will allow the chief to speak out on issues that might run counter to the positions of the politicians. The process of silencing chiefs in today's America is almost complete.

Cooperating with Police

7. *The American Public Needs to Grow Up.* At some point, the public is going to have to adopt a more realistic view of the police. It needs to recognize what we are and what we aren't. The people pass laws to control traffic and pay the police to enforce those laws. Then, when we stop them for a violation, they get mad at *us.* . . .

The public also sadly lacks perspective. In the case of Rodney King, an ex-con who was driving while under the influence of alcohol—going way beyond the speed limit, being chased for several miles by police units with red lights flashing and sirens blaring—four officers were charged with improper use of force in subduing him. Though the officers were subsequently acquitted, no one in the LAPD has tried to defend what those officers did. Yet the media's lopsided reporting (King was usually identified as "motorist Rodney King," evoking a picture of a guy just out for a spin) resulted in many people damning the *entire* LAPD. . . .

Rodney King should never have been hit fifty-six times; yet many of the blows struck him were correctly placed so as not to cause serious injury, exactly as we teach at the Academy. Even in a situation where officers act entirely appropriately, as they did *not* in the King episode, when you are trying to subdue a moving, often violent suspect, one or two blows may miss their mark. This is the reality. It is the reality of police work in a world of guns and violence and sociopathic behavior that is almost beyond human understanding.

Some will say this is a chief who is minimizing police violence; I am not. I am just stating the facts. Judgments about the police come too quickly, too harshly, too often. The public is too quick to jump from the particular to the general, and there are always those in the media and in the political world willing to help the public make that jump.

In addition, the public must come to terms with what we do. Citizens ought to know they have a partnership with the police. When an officer stops a citizen, the citizen should not mistake demands for discourtesy. He should cooperate. At the same time, the officer absolutely must explain—with courtesy—why the person has been stopped. . . .

The Best Possible Job

Over the years I have seen the best and the worst in police officers. But in comparison to others in government, you get more dedication, commitment, and overall ability to get a job done. In addition, the disciplinary system under which police officers operate has no peer in or out of government. We are tougher, as we should be, on police officers for their misconduct on and off the job. When a citizen is arrested for drunk driving, he pays his fine and does his time and that's it. When a police officer is arrested, he pays his fine, does his time, and then must face severe discipline by the department.

We don't flinch from the extra demands placed upon us, but we do believe the public should take that into consideration. We are not the enemy—we truly belong to you. We will do your bidding and try to do the best possible job.

Evaluating Sources of Information

When historians study and interpret past events, they use two kinds of sources: primary and secondary. Primary sources are eyewitness accounts. For example, a judge who has written an editorial about the problems confronting her courtroom is a primary source. An article in a newspaper that used the judge's editorial to describe the conditions of courtrooms in the United States would be a secondary source. Primary and secondary sources may be decades or even hundreds of years old, and often historians find that the sources offer conflicting and contradictory information. To fully evaluate documents and assess their accuracy, historians analyze the credibility of the documents' authors and, in the case of secondary sources, analyze the credibility of the information the authors used.

Historians are not the only people who encounter conflicting information, however. Anyone who reads a daily newspaper, watches television, or just talks to different people will encounter many different views. Writers and speakers use sources of information to support their own statements. Thus, critical thinkers, just like historians, must question the writer's or speaker's sources of information as well as the writer or speaker.

While there are many criteria that can be applied to assess the accuracy of a primary or secondary source, for this activity you will be asked to apply three. For each source listed on the following page, ask yourself the following questions: First, did the person actually see or participate in the event he or she is reporting? This will help you determine the credibility of the information—an eyewitness to an event is an extremely valuable source. Second, does the person have a vested interest in the report? Assessing the person's social status, professional affiliations, nationality, and religious or political beliefs will be helpful in considering this question. By evaluating this you will be able to determine how objective the person's report may be. Third, how qualified is the author to be making the statements he or she is making? Consider what the person's profession is and how he or she might know about the event. Someone who has spent years being involved with or studying the issue may be able to offer more information than someone who simply is offering an uneducated opinion; for example, a politician or layperson.

Keeping the above criteria in mind, imagine you are writing a research paper on criminal justice reform in the United States. You decide to cite an equal number of primary and secondary sources. Listed below are several sources that may be useful for your research. *Place a P next to those descriptions you believe are primary sources. Place an S next to those descriptions you believe are secondary sources.* Next, based on the above criteria, *rank the primary sources, assigning the number (1) to what appears to be the most valuable, (2) to the source likely to be the second-most valuable, and so on, until all the primary sources are ranked. Then rank the secondary sources, again using the above criteria.*

		Rank in
P or S		*Importance*
_____	1. A book about prejudice in the criminal justice system that refers to accounts given by minorities.	_____
_____	2. Viewpoint one in this chapter.	_____
_____	3. A *Time* magazine article about America's overburdened court system.	_____
_____	4. The Sixth Amendment to the U.S. Constitution, which guarantees an individual the right to counsel.	_____
_____	5. The U.S. Supreme Court case of *Miranda v. Arizona*.	_____
_____	6. An article in the *New York Times* which discusses different opinions about how to punish criminal offenders.	_____
_____	7. A speech by former U.S. Supreme Court justice Thurgood Marshall criticizing the Supreme Court for taking away criminals' rights.	_____
_____	8. A *Newsweek* article about victim/offender mediation.	_____
_____	9. A college graduation speech by a federal judge that describes how the criminal justice system should be reformed.	_____
_____	10. An article in the *New York Times* that discusses several reforms in the criminal justice system suggested by legal experts.	_____
_____	11. Daryl Gates's book *Chief: My Life in the LAPD*, which offers his suggestions on how to improve the criminal justice system.	_____

Periodical Bibliography

The following articles have been selected to supplement the diverse views presented in this chapter.

George M. Anderson — "Sentencing, Race, and the Poor," *America*, December 29, 1990.

Allan C. Brownfeld — "Ramblings," *The St. Croix Review*, October 1990. Available from PO Box 244, Stillwater, MN 55082.

Lawrence H. Cooke — "The Courts Belong to the People," *Vital Speeches of the Day*, April 15, 1988.

Alan Ellis — "A Glaring Contrast: Criminal Justice Black and White," *The Wall Street Journal*, May 14, 1992.

Barney Frank — "Race and Crime: Let's Talk Sense," *The New York Times*, January 13, 1992.

Irving R. Kaufman — "Speedy Justice—At What Cost?" *The New York Times*, May 1, 1990.

Roger Koopman — "One Angry Man," *The New American*, February 12, 1991. Available from The Review of the News Inc., 770 Westhill Blvd., Appleton, WI 54915.

Stephanie Mencimer — "Black Robe," *The Washington Monthly*, April 1992.

Terry C. Muck — "A Not-Too Severe Mercy," *Christianity Today*, July 14, 1989.

Salim Muwakkil — "The 'Just Us' System Is an Offense to a Defender," *In These Times*, July 5-18, 1989.

Graeme Newman — "Turning Bad into Good," *Chronicles*, May 1992. Available from 934 N. Main St., Rockford, IL 61103.

Neal Peirce — "More Arrests, Less Deterrence: A Criminal Justice System Gone Awry," *Liberal Opinion Week*, January 20, 1992. Available from 108 E. Fifth St., Vinton, IA 52349.

Charles B. Rangel — "Our Criminal Justice System Needs Reform," *Trial*, April 1992.

The Wall Street Journal — "Frontier Justice," June 16, 1988.

Do the Rights of the Accused Undermine the Criminal Justice System?

Chapter Preface

The U.S. Constitution guarantees each individual protection against the state when he or she is arrested. These rights, which are intended to protect the accused from indiscriminate prosecution by the government, include the right to be informed of the reason for the arrest, the right to a lawyer, and the right to be protected against unreasonable searches and seizures. While most Americans value the wisdom of protecting the accused, some critics believe accused rights go too far and may allow guilty people to go free.

These critics contend that courts have expanded accused rights beyond those guaranteed by the Constitution. One example cited by critics is the exclusionary rule. This rule prevents police officers from obtaining evidence without a search warrant or without a strong reason to believe a crime has been committed. Some legal experts believe that the rule goes beyond its intent and actually prevents officers from gathering evidence that would convict criminals. For example, in 1979, Osborne Sheppard was convicted of killing Sandra Boulware. Bloody boots, a hairpiece, and wire fragments were found and used to convict Sheppard. His conviction, however, was overturned because a judge who issued a warrant to police failed to explicitly describe the evidence the police seized. This was viewed as a miscarriage of justice by some, who blame the exclusionary rule for the release of many criminals such as Sheppard. Protesting the rule as a burden on police, former chief deputy attorney general of Delaware Charles Brandt states, "The exclusionary rule is a judge-made rule of courtroom evidence, not a constitutional right. We need to protest the way the Constitution has been nitpicked by judges and the truth banished from the courthouse." The rule, Brandt concludes, allows criminals to be set free.

Defenders of the exclusionary rule and similar protections for the accused believe that such protections safeguard the accused from the enormous power of the government. Advocates also point out that these rights have created procedures that keep police from abusing their power. Law student Myron Orfield, noted that a Chicago narcotics squad opposed eliminating the rule because it kept them from indiscriminately searching a home or business merely because they believed evidence may be hidden there. The exclusionary rule makes police "stop and think before they search—exactly what the Fourth Amendment wants them to do," says Richard Uviller, a Columbia University law professor.

The accused have rights that protect them from being unfairly convicted. The authors in this chapter debate whether these rights impede justice in the United States.

"The rights of the accused often mean very little because they are ignored by police, prosecutors, and even judges."

The Rights of the Accused Must Be Zealously Protected

David Luban

A primary goal of the criminal justice system should be to protect the rights of the accused, according to David Luban. In the following viewpoint, Luban argues that the state is a powerful entity that must be restrained in its attempt to prosecute the accused. He contends that the rights of the accused help curtail the state's power, prevent unjust prosecutions, and protect civil liberties. Luban is a law professor at the University of Maryland School of Law in Baltimore.

As you read, consider the following questions:

1. How does the system prevent the accused from enjoying their rights, according to Luban?
2. What is the real purpose behind the ruling in *Gideon v. Wainwright*, according to the author?
3. What two things does Luban contend the right to counsel accomplishes?

Criminal defense is a very special case, in which the zealous advocate serves atypical social goals. The point is one of political theory. The goal of zealous advocacy in criminal defense is to curtail the power of the state over its citizens. We want to handicap the state in its power even legitimately to punish us, for we believe as a matter of political theory and historical experience that if the state is not handicapped or restrained *ex ante*, our political and civil liberties are jeopardized. Power-holders are inevitably tempted to abuse the criminal justice system to persecute political opponents, and overzealous police will trample civil liberties in the name of crime prevention and order. To guard against these dangers, we protect our rights by in effect overprotecting them.

A Facade of Justice

The idea that criminal procedures should overprotect us against the state is reflected in numerous features of the law—the so-called "rights of the accused"—which it will be useful to review briefly. Before doing so, however, an important caution is in order. The most important real-world fact about our criminal justice system is that persons accused of crimes enjoy no advantages whatever, no matter how many rights the courts and legislatures have apportioned them. For in the overwhelming majority of cases, they have no opportunity to exercise any of their rights—instead, these rights are plea-bargained away. The practice of plea-bargaining is extremely troubling on both moral and political grounds. John Langbein has noted that it may actually be a byproduct of the paper advantage enjoyed by the accused: because the accused have robust rights, formally, it would be too expensive and time-consuming actually to permit them to exercise those rights, and as a result defendants are compelled to bargain them away. Langbein analogizes this to the antique law of procedure, according to which one could be convicted only if one had confessed. Granting the accused such a colossal advantage meant that convictions could be obtained only by torturing a confession out of the accused. Plea-bargaining is the modern version of torture.

It is also important to notice that the zealous advocate provided for in theory is not so zealous in practice: as a repeat player in the criminal justice system, the defense lawyer has an interest in playing ball with the prosecution and encouraging the client to plea-bargain.

Finally, the rights of the accused often mean very little because they are ignored by police, prosecutors, and even judges. Supreme Court decisions in the mid-1980s permitting illegally obtained evidence to be used if the police believed in good faith that they were acting legally amount to a backhanded admission that even after decades of experience, the idea that the accused have rights has failed to rub off on many enforcement personnel.

Thus, our current arguments about zealous advocacy in criminal defense concern a utopian ideal, whereas the harsh reality is that criminal defendants too often receive little more than the bum's rush into prison. To analyze the adversary system in the context of criminal defense we must nevertheless concern ourselves with the ideal—the law in books and not in action—because otherwise there is no adversary system to discuss. For the quickie plea-bargain, conducted as indifferently as a back-alley drug deal, has nothing to do with adversary advocacy; nor, of course, does the practice of law as a confidence game in which the defense lawyer needs and gets the judge's cooperation in imprisoning his own client until the bill is paid. To discuss the adversary system we must raise our eyes above its sordid caricature. Nor is this completely unrealistic: for it is also true that in public defender offices throughout the United States, and even in that portion of the private bar devoted to penny-ante criminal defense, zealous, conscientious, and principled advocates can be found. As Raymond Chandler says, "Down these mean streets a man must go who is not himself mean, who is neither tarnished nor afraid." It happens sometimes.

Keeping the State at Arm's Length

Let us turn, then, to the law in books—the rights of the accused. The accused is presumed innocent until proven guilty, and the standard of evidence in criminal trials is proof beyond a reasonable doubt, the highest standard to be found in the law. Evidence obtained illegally is excluded because of our fear that otherwise the police will violate our rights so they can get the goods. Moreover, public prosecutors are held (on paper at any rate) to a standard of candor in dealing with their adversaries that is not mirrored in the duties of defense counsels:

> A public prosecutor or other government lawyer in criminal litigation shall make timely disclosure to counsel for the defendant, or to the defendant if he has no counsel, of the existence of evidence, known to the prosecutor or other government lawyer, that tends to negate the guilt of the accused, mitigate the degree of the offense, or reduce the punishment. [American Bar Association Code DP. 7—103 (B)]

Criminal defendants have a right not to incriminate themselves by testifying, and their other rights to due process of law are reflected in cases that are almost household names—*Miranda* [and] *Mapp*.

One of these household names is *Gideon—Gideon v. Wainwright*, decided in 1963, which held that anyone accused of a felony for which a conviction might result in imprisonment is entitled to legal counsel at government expense. It might be thought that the purpose of this decision is to balance the adversary scales, that is, to perfect the adversary process, and not (as I am arguing) to overprotect our rights by hobbling the state in its enforcement of the criminal code. To a certain extent, it is true that balance is at stake here; but balance and overprotection are complementary rather than mutually exclusive goals, and two considerations suggest that perfecting the adversary process is not the whole story.

A Landmark Case

In *Gideon v. Wainwright* the highest Court in the land "reach[ed] down" to hear the plea of a fifty-two-year-old drifter, an outcast from society. The story of how lawyers and judges handled Clarence Gideon's handwritten misspelled appeal is worth remembering. As Anthony Lewis states, the "care, the vision, the imagination" of the attorneys appointed by the Supreme Court to represent Gideon on his appeal makes one "proud of law and lawyers in this country." The simple elegance of the majority opinion written by Justice Hugo Black, is also impressive. In that opinion Justice Black proclaimed the "obvious truth [that] any person hauled into court, who is too poor to hire a lawyer, cannot be assured of a fair trial unless counsel is provided for him."

Michael B. Mushlin, *Pace Law Review*, Spring 1990.

First, the right to counsel exists in the context of the other rules and rights I have just enumerated; and most of these can only be understood as attempts to prevent the state from obtaining even justified convictions by unacceptably invasive means. The reasonable doubt standard of proof, for example, or the exclusionary rule, or the right against self-incrimination have nothing to do with balancing the adversary process. They have to do with keeping the state's police power at arm's length.

Second, the defense counsel is not simply provided—she is held to a standard of zeal that is hard to explain as simply an attempt to balance the adversary scales, because, on paper at least, the prosecutor is directed to restrain her own zeal in the name of justice. The defense lawyer, although she is paid for by the state, works solely for the client. In contrast to many other legal systems, in our system she is supposed to be wholly independent from the prosecution, promoting the client's interests even at the expense of the common good. The defense lawyer, when she performs her role properly, is a wild card injected into the proceeding by the state and intended by the state to function as its own nemesis.

All this suggests that "balancing the adversary scales" is not the main point of providing the criminal accused with a zealous advocate, though it is certainly one point of doing so. The political argument for zealous criminal defense does not claim that the adversary system is the best way of obtaining justice. It claims just the opposite, that this process is the best way of impeding justice in the name of more fundamental political ends, namely keeping the government's hands off people. Nothing, of course, is wrong with that; indeed, I believe that Lord Henry Brougham's imperative may well hold in criminal defense. My point is merely that criminal defense is an exceptional part of the legal system, one that aims at the people's protection from the state rather than at accurate outcomes.

"The law effectively surrendered to the criminals when courts forced cops and prosecutors to fight with one arm held behind their backs. "

Zealous Protection of the Rights of the Accused Undermines Justice

L. Gordon Crovitz

The courts have given too many rights and protections to criminal defendants, L. Gordon Crovitz states in the following viewpoint. Crovitz argues that the focus on the rights of the accused allows too many criminals to be released on technicalities and puts citizens at the mercy of these violent criminals. He contends that cops and prosecutors should focus on determining the guilt or innocence of a suspect rather than on the suspect's rights. Crovitz, a lawyer and assistant editorial page editor of the *Wall Street Journal*, writes the newspaper's weekly column "Rule of Law."

As you read, consider the following questions:

1. What did the case of *Papachristou v. City of Jacksonville* do for American cities, according to Crovitz?
2. How has the increase in the rights of the accused affected police, according to the author?
3. What are criminal prosecutors doing since violent criminals are able to avoid prosecution, according to Crovitz?

L. Gordon Crovitz, "How Law Destroys Order," *National Review*, February 11, 1991. Copyright © 1991 by National Review, Inc., 150 E. 35th St., New York, NY 10016. Reprinted by permission.

The phrase "law and order" implies cause and effect. The United States is now discovering the corollary, to wit: A legal system that fails to protect order signals flaws in the law itself. We now have a legal system that creates chaos and disdains order. As a result, criminals rule urban streets. . . .

Any law-and-order movement today requires a focus both wide and deep. We must recapture the most fundamental idea in our jurisprudence—the rule of law. Our laws must be fair, based on common sense, and easily understood by the citizens who are expected to live under them; they must punish the guilty and protect the innocent; and they must be molded to the needs of society and not to any group's arbitrary standards. In particular, now that the results are in, it is time to end liberalism's social experimentation through the courts. An emerging intellectual conservative majority on the highest courts marks a change in direction, but whether it will mean a renewed conservative approach to the law remains to be seen.

Opening the Door to Crime

Recall how police officers once enforced the law. If they saw a suspicious character hanging out on the street, they would routinely haul him in on vagrancy or loitering charges. These statutes were sometimes abused to harass minorities, but when properly used they had the virtue of permitting the police to prevent the street/park/schoolyard activity that facilitates drug dealing.

The law effectively surrendered to the criminals when courts forced cops and prosecutors to fight with one arm held behind their backs. The 1972 case of *Papachristou v. City of Jacksonville*, written by Justice William O. Douglas, is a perfect example. Several local toughs were arrested under a city ordinance against vagrants, defined as "rogues and vagabonds, . . . common drunkards, common night thieves, . . . persons wandering or strolling around from place to place without any lawful purpose or object. . . ." One of the defendants had packets of heroin; others had long criminal records. The Justices reversed all the vagrancy convictions and invalidated these laws for hundreds of cities.

"The implicit presumption in these generalized vagrancy standards—that crime is nipped in the bud—is too extravagant to deserve extended treatment," Justice Douglas wrote, despite acknowledging that "of course, vagrancy statutes are useful to the police." Instead, he wrote an essay championing the alternative lifestyle now on exhibit in every urban area.

Justice Douglas cited a former governor of Puerto Rico to the effect that loafing "was a virtue in his commonwealth and that it should be encouraged." "Persons 'wandering or strolling' from place to place have been extolled by Walt Whitman and Vachel

Lindsay," Justice Douglas wrote. "We know that sleepless people often walk at night, perhaps hopeful that sleep-inducing relaxation will result."

There was no evidence of the police arresting rambling poets or somnambulists. The Justices waved away evidence that from Elizabethan times such laws had been crucial to maintaining order. After years of living with the results, black community groups across the country are now agitating for renewed vagrancy laws as the best hope for closing down open-air drug markets. But when local leaders got Alexandria, Virginia, to pass new prohibitions on loitering, the American Civil Liberties Union (ACLU) persuaded a federal judge to invalidate the law. Legal liberalism has been reduced to fighting community empowerment.

"Of course the defendant wasn't read his rights immediately, your Honor. He was captured by a police dog!"

When the police arrest a suspect and he confesses, this is now the beginning, not the end, of the case. Volumes of exclusionary rules now suppress evidence of wrongdoing, from voluntary confessions to unambiguous evidence of weapons and drugs. Remember the Shia Amal militiamen U.S. forces lured into a trap and arrested a few years ago? A federal district court suppressed the confession by one of the militiamen that he had blown up an airliner on the grounds that the *Miranda* warning he got after he was arrested in the Mediterranean had three words misspelled in Arabic. (An appeals court later allowed the confessions.)

Many years ago, Judge Benjamin Nathan Cardozo wrote that it is absurd that "the criminal is to go free because the constable blundered." Yet even the new conservative majority on the Supreme Court seems intent on expanding the exclusionary rule. In an opinion by Justice Anthony Kennedy, the Court quashed a confession to two murders because the defendant's lawyer was not in the room when he confessed. What began as a way to ensure that the police do not coerce confessions has become a legal game in which defendants are protected from their voluntary confessions. One-third of the time that prosecutors fail to bring drug cases, it's because of exclusionary-rule problems.

One predictable result is that we have many fewer police officers on the street. Why bother paying for police who are destined to fail? New York lawyer Adam Walinsky has collected the data. Thirty years ago there were three police officers for every violent crime; now there are three violent crimes for every police officer. The ratio of violent crimes to police officers is an excellent measure of the crime of a city. The recent ratio for San Diego is 5.4; Boston, 6.1; Atlanta, 9.6; Oakland, 10.7; and East St. Louis, 26.7.

It may be only human nature that top law-enforcement officials have reacted to their failure to control violent crime by shifting their sights to crimes they can still investigate and prosecute. At the federal level, former Attorney General Dick Thornburgh speaks of "crime in the suites," implying a moral relativism between white-collar crime and violent crime. At the same time that Mr. Thornburgh announced he would disband the long-standing Strike Forces on Organized Crime, he created new Task Forces on Securities and Commodities Fraud. The frustration at the inability to confront violent crime created what Tom Wolfe's *Bonfire of the Vanities* referred to as the search for the "Great White [Collar] Defendant." Michael Milken can be brought to his knees, using the RICO [Racketeer Influenced and Corrupt Organization] law, for "crimes" that are still mysterious, but muggers, rapists, and murderers are routinely set free.

People worry more about thugs than about shady accountants. A survey by *National Law Journal*/Lexis asked which crime should rank the highest for law enforcement; 47 per cent of the respondents said drug dealing, 32 per cent said muggings and rapes, 11 per cent said racketeering, 3 per cent said white-collar crimes. The same point was made in this hypothetical: An armed robber gets away with $5,000 from a bank. So does an embezzler. What sentences are appropriate? Streets *v.* suites was no contest: Nearly half would have put the armed robber away for more than ten years, while only 12 per cent thought the white-collar embezzler should serve more than ten years. While prosecutors of course must prosecute white-collar abuses, this is no substitute for fighting against violent crime.

=====

"In Miranda v. Arizona . . . *the Constitution can be read to create such a dubious privilege:* a right of criminals to conceal their crimes."

=====

The Miranda Rule Undermines the Criminal Justice System

Paul Savoy

In the 1966 Supreme Court case of *Miranda v. Arizona,* the Court ruled that when making an arrest, police officers must inform suspects of their constitutional rights, including the right to remain silent and to have an attorney present during questioning. In the following viewpoint, Paul Savoy argues that the right to remain silent is a protection for innocent defendants against self-incrimination if they are accused of a crime. *Miranda,* he concludes, has weakened the criminal justice system by allowing guilty suspects to remain silent about their crimes. Savoy, a former prosecutor and law professor, is writing a book about the U.S. Supreme Court.

As you read, consider the following questions:

1. What does the story of Edgar Smith exemplify for Savoy?
2. Under what conditions should the court be allowed to use a defendant's confession to a crime, according to the author?
3. What two revisions should be incorporated into the *Miranda* warnings, according to Savoy?

From Paul Savoy, "When Criminal Rights Go Wrong," *The Washington Monthly,* December 1989. Reprinted with permission from *The Washington Monthly*. Copyright by The Washington Monthly Company, 1611 Connecticut Avenue NW, Washington, DC 20009. (202) 462-0128.

Having provided the framework for what was surely the most ambitious and idealistic effort in the history of the Supreme Court to bring the Constitution to bear upon flagrant abuses in the administration of criminal justice, liberals have become willing to accept the assumptions and principles of that 1960s revolution as dogma beyond accountability to serious moral or intellectual inquiry. Deeper and more mature reflection on the history and purpose of the procedural guarantees of the Constitution—including most prominently . . . the Fifth Amendment privilege against compulsory self-incrimination—will show that fundamental rights were not intended, and should not be construed, to protect the guilty.

A Freed Murderer

In 1957, Edgar Smith was convicted of murdering a 15-year-old girl and sentenced to die in the electric chair. High school sophomore Vickie Zielinski had disappeared on her way home from visiting a friend, and her battered body was found the next day in a sand pit on the outskirts of the small New Jersey town where she lived. Her skull had been crushed with a 44-pound boulder, leaving a gaping hole in her head and her brains scattered along the bank.

In 1969, the Supreme Court ordered a hearing to determine if incriminating statements Smith made to police had been obtained in violation of his constitutional rights. Although Smith acknowledged that he had not been mistreated by the police officer who conducted the interrogation, and three psychiatrists testified that the statements were "the result of his free will and rational choice," a federal court in New Jersey ruled the statements were inadmissible because they were obtained under "coercive" circumstances: Smith had not been advised of his right to remain silent or his right to counsel, and his interrogation had extended over a period of more than 10 hours. After 14 years on Death Row, Smith, who continued to assert his innocence, was released from prison because, without his statements, there was insufficient evidence to retry him for first-degree murder.

Five years after his release, in 1976, Smith finally did confess to killing Vickie Zielinski—at a trial in San Diego in which he was convicted of kidnapping and attempted murder after abducting another woman and stabbing her with a six-inch butcher knife as she struggled to escape. "Don't ask me why I did it," Smith later wrote from San Quentin Prison regarding the San Diego attack. "Ask those self-righteous public servants why they gave me the opportunity to do it.". . .

After being arrested at his home in Phoenix, Arizona, Ernesto Miranda was picked out of a lineup by an 18-year-old victim as the man who had kidnapped and brutally raped her. Two officers then took Miranda into a separate room to question him. At first he denied his guilt, but after two hours of interrogation, he gave a detailed oral confession and then wrote out and signed a brief statement in which he admitted and described the crime. Although unmarked by any of the traditional indicia of coercion, Miranda's oral and written confessions were held inadmissible because the police had failed to advise him of his right to remain silent and his right to a lawyer. As Justice John Harlan suggested, in dissenting with three other members of the Warren Court from the majority's 1966 ruling in *Miranda v. Arizona*, "one is entitled to feel astonished" that the Constitution can be read to create such a dubious privilege: *a right of criminals to conceal their crimes.*

THE HANDCUFFS ARE ON THE WRONG MAN

To be sure, the law has long regarded torture and other blatant forms of coercion as unlawful means of obtaining a confession, for the reasons that a coerced confession is likely to be untrustworthy and that the use of physical brutality offends civilized standards of fair play and decency. But when a confession is indisputably true, and the police have not used the blackjack or the third-degree, the reason for the privilege is more difficult to fathom. This is not to dispute the wisdom of the Court's decision in *Miranda* requiring that, before questioning, people in police custody be advised of their rights under the Fifth and Sixth Amendments. A decision about whether to invoke a constitutional right should be the product of an informed and independent choice, and advising a person that he has such a right contributes to his freedom to choose.

The more obvious question, but one that is rarely asked about *Miranda*, is why a criminal suspect should have a right to remain silent in the first place. Even as conservative a critic of *Miranda* as former Attorney General Edwin Meese conceded that "if a person doesn't want to answer, that's [his] right." However, as Judge Henry Friendly once observed, "no parent would teach such a doctrine to his children." The guilty, according to the moral standards that prevail outside the courtroom, should own up to their guilt, while the innocent, one would think, have nothing to fear by telling the truth.

Protecting the Innocent

Describing the complex of values embodied in the Fifth Amendment privilege against compulsory self-incrimination, Chief Justice Warren, in his opinion for the Court in *Miranda*, explained that the privilege has come to be recognized in part as an individual's "right to a private enclave where he may lead a private life." Elsewhere, the Court has said of the privilege that it is "intended to shield the guilty and imprudent as well as the innocent."

Despite the Court's confident pronouncements, however, the conclusion that a person who has committed a rape or any other crime has a privacy interest in not answering a police officer's questions is supported neither by the historical record nor by evolving standards of fair play and decency. The story of the historic struggle for the privilege as a protest in behalf of the guilty and the innocent alike against the abuses of inquisitorial methods of interrogation is largely a fairy tale. . . .

The privilege against self-incrimination was originally conceived as an essentially spiritual principle that permitted a person who had a conscientious belief in his innocence to assert what was tantamount to a right of passive resistance against an unjust law or a false accusation. The modern use of the privilege that best exemplifies its original purpose was the exercise of the Fifth Amendment during the McCarthy era. Given the Cold War climate of the fifties, a Supreme Court that could not quite bring itself to declare that active membership in the Communist Party was protected by the First Amendment could nevertheless find in the procedural guarantee of the Fifth Amendment a politically safe way of permitting people of conscience to resist legislative inquisitions into left-wing departures from the established democratic faith.

Even when freedom of conscience is not at stake, the privilege operates to protect the innocent. Contrary to popular belief, an innocent person may have a great deal to lose by telling the truth. For example, an innocent person, by admitting certain elements missing from the prosecution's case, such as his presence at the scene of the crime, or that he owned the murder weapon, or even that it was he who fatally stabbed the victim (though in self-defense), has a legitimate concern that by telling the truth he may contribute to his being convicted of a crime he did not in fact commit or for which he had sufficient justification. The right to remain silent thus reflects our unwillingness as a society to permit an *innocent* person to become the instrument of his own conviction.

Revising *Miranda*

Given the purpose of the privilege to protect the innocent and those who hold a conscientious belief in their innocence, a revised set of *Miranda* warnings that would be more consistent with the history of the privilege, as well as contemporary standards of fairness and justice, should include, in addition to the existing admonitions regarding the right to consult with an attorney, the following: 1) If you believe you are innocent, you are not required to make a statement, or to answer any questions; 2) If you are guilty, you have a legal duty to answer questions and to state truthfully the circumstances concerning your commission of the offense with which you are charged.

> "Miranda vs. Arizona *means that information about our Constitution is no longer rationed on the basis of wealth, experience or education.*"

The Miranda Rule Does Not Undermine the Criminal Justice System

Peter D. Baird

Peter D. Baird, an attorney in Phoenix, Arizona, was one of the lawyers who represented Ernesto Miranda, the defendant in the *Miranda v. Arizona* case. In the following article, Baird argues that the *Miranda* rule is important because it protects the constitutional rights of the accused. He contends that *Miranda* is a minor inconvenience for police and does not hamper the criminal justice system's ability to convict those accused of crimes.

As you read, consider the following questions:

1. Why should it be difficult to arrest someone, according to Baird?
2. What do studies point out about *Miranda*'s effect on criminal arrests and trials, according to the author?
3. Why does *Miranda* still make sense today, according to Baird?

Peter D. Baird, "Critics Must Confess, *Miranda* Was the Right Decision," *The Wall Street Journal*, June 13, 1991. Reprinted with permission of *The Wall Street Journal*, © 1991 Dow Jones & Company, Inc. All rights reserved.

The *Miranda* warning. Civil libertarians have praised it, critics such as the *Wall Street Journal* have condemned it, and police officers recite it thousands of times a day.

It was the result of the Supreme Court's most famous criminal decision, made 25 years ago. In its 5-to-4 decision in *Miranda vs. Arizona*, perhaps its most famous criminal case, the court held that arrested suspects must be advised of their constitutional rights before their confessions to police could be presented at trial.

After laboring for years with subjective and variable criteria, the court in *Miranda* formulated objective and uniform standards and required that specific, constitutional information be read to persons in custody. Only when suspects understand their rights can they waive those rights. For years, critics have denounced *Miranda* for blocking confessions from unwarned suspects and for mandating that constitutional information be given to citizens when they need it most—upon their arrest. According to its detractors, *Miranda* undermines the criminal justice system because police investigations have been compromised; law enforcement has become more difficult; and dangerous criminals have gone unprosecuted or have been turned loose on a "technicality." Met head-on, these criticisms are wrong or are hugely exaggerated.

Preserving Constitutional Rights

In almost every instance, *Miranda* does not affect methods of pre-arrest investigation and detection because the court's decision applies only to suspects in custody. For this reason, police need not read "*Miranda* warnings" to witnesses, third parties or even suspects themselves until they are actually under arrest. *Miranda* only crimps police when they conduct custodial interrogations.

Has *Miranda* made law enforcement more difficult? Of course it has. For 25 years, police have been forced to read constitutional rights to hundreds of thousands of suspects, without word games, lies or qualifiers. If the arresting officers are not professional enough to read the *Miranda* warnings in the first place, and if the only evidence is the unwarned suspect's confession, then the prosecutor's case will be stillborn. However:

• Reading suspects their rights is hardly more than a nettlesome inconvenience for police. And under the Constitution, it is supposed to be difficult to deprive citizens of their liberty.

• Unlike other constitutional protections such as trial by jury, *Miranda*'s "burden" on the justice system can be shouldered quickly and inexpensively. It takes only seconds for trained officers to read *Miranda* warnings.

• All *Miranda* did was "constitutionalize" what the FBI had been doing for years before—read arrested suspects their rights. Surely the FBI would not have engaged in a practice that compromised effective law enforcement.

Does Not Stifle Justice

As the Supreme Court ruled in 1971 in *Harris vs. New York*, *Miranda* does not give suspects a license to lie. If police fail to warn a suspect properly and the suspect confesses, the police can then read the suspect a *Miranda* warning. If the suspect at that point changes his mind and denies the crime, the original confession can still be presented at trial to "impeach" or contradict the suspect's denial.

The Miranda Rule

1. You have a right to remain silent.

2. If you give up the right to remain silent, anything you do say can and will be used in court against you.

3. You have the right to speak with an attorney of your choice before questioning, and to have the attorney present during questioning.

4. If you cannot afford an attorney, one will be appointed for you by the court prior to any questioning, if you so desire. The attorney will not cost you anything, the services are free.

---

1. Question: Do you understand each of these rights that I have explained to you?

2. Question: Having in mind and understanding your rights as I have told you, are you willing to talk to me?

San Diego, California, Police Department, 1992.

But what about the principal law-and-order argument: that *Miranda* has permitted dangerous criminals to go free? Has this "judicially invented technicality" stifled the rate of confession, indictment and conviction? The realities are these:

• According to John Kaplan of the Stanford Law School in the November 1987 issue of the *American Bar Association Journal*, suspects confess just as easily when they are given their *Miranda* warnings as when they are not. The more polite and professional the police, the more inclined suspects seem to be to talk, explain or unburden themselves.

• Empirical studies bear Prof. Kaplan out. In 1981, the *Ohio State Law Journal* reported that field research has demonstrated that *Miranda* has not significantly affected the number or rate of confessions, convictions or "clearances," confessions to crimes "cleared" but not prosecuted.

• Once prosecutors have confessions in hand, remarkably few founder at trial. *Newsweek* reported in July 1988 that fewer than 1% of criminal cases are thrown out because of defective confessions. Of that 1%, only a fraction were voided because of noncompliance with *Miranda*. A 1983 study of 260 arrests for robbery in California found that no evidence at all was excluded on *Miranda* grounds. Another analysis of 2,804 cases in 38 U.S. attorneys' offices revealed that only 4.4% of defendants even filed motions to suppress their own confessions at trial.

Miranda Favored

• Given these studies and statistics, it is not surprising that the overwhelming bulk of informed opinion affirmatively favors *Miranda* or, at least, finds its impact to be neutral. Both former Justice Tom Clark, who dissented in *Miranda*, and former Chief Justice Warren Burger, whom President Nixon appointed to the Supreme Court, have expressed the view—in a 1989 issue of the *University of Chicago Law Review*—that *Miranda* has not had a negative impact on criminal prosecutions. And this acceptance is not restricted to lofty judges or cloistered academics.

• Perhaps the best example of how the *Miranda* decision did not turn loose the criminal population is Ernesto Miranda himself. After the Supreme Court reversed his conviction, Miranda was re-tried without his confession being presented in court and he was convicted again and re-sentenced, all without enjoying a single day of freedom. Indeed, because of the scrutiny the Arizona Parole Board gave its most famous petitioner, Miranda probably served more, not less, time in prison as a result of the Supreme Court's landmark ruling in his own case.

Protecting Everyone's Rights

Miranda is anything but a mindless "technicality." Even if everything its critics said were true, *Miranda* would still make compelling constitutional sense. It all comes down to this: The organized criminal, the educated and the affluent are almost always aware of their constitutional guarantees when they confront the state in a criminal showdown, but there are literally millions of functionally illiterate, poor and uneducated citizens who do not know what their rights are when the cuffs snap on, the pressure is applied or the night sticks strike. More than anything else, *Miranda vs. Arizona* means that information about our Constitution is no longer rationed on the basis of wealth, experience or education.

"The exclusionary rule vindicates only the rights of criminals."

Excluding Illegally Seized Evidence Handicaps Criminal Justice

U.S. Department of Justice

The U.S. Supreme Court in two leading cases, *Weeks v. United States* and *Mapp v. Ohio*, ruled that criminal investigators cannot violate an individual's Fourth Amendment right against illegal searches and seizures. The Court said illegally obtained evidence of a crime cannot be used in court to convict a defendant. In the following viewpoint, the U.S. Department of Justice argues that this rule, known as the exclusionary rule, hinders the administration of criminal justice. The department's investigation finds that the rule burdens police with excessive procedures and that prosecutors must set guilty people free because they cannot use evidence that would prove their guilt. The Department of Justice compiles statistics on crime and the criminal justice system.

As you read, consider the following questions:

1. What are four criticisms of the exclusionary rule, according to the department?
2. How does the exclusionary rule favor criminal defendants, according to the author?
3. What does the department suggest the Supreme Court do to make the exclusionary rule less of a burden on the states?

From the U.S. Department of Justice report to the attorney general on the search and seizure exclusionary rule "Truth in Criminal Justice," Report no. 2, Office of Legal Policy, February 26, 1986.

The fourth amendment guarantees the "right of the people to be secure in their persons, houses, papers, and effects, against unreasonable searches and seizures." This guaranty is not self-executing, however, and the courts and criminal justice systems in this country have long been bedeviled by questions concerning appropriate methods of ensuring its observance. As a result of the Supreme Court's decisions in *Weeks v. United States* and *Mapp v. Ohio*, the method principally relied upon today is a judicially created rule excluding from criminal trials evidence obtained in violation of the defendant's fourth amendment rights.

The search and seizure exclusionary rule is subject to a number of well-founded criticisms. First, the rule has no support in the "original intent or meaning" of the Framers of the Constitution. Second, the validity of the rule's deterrence rationale has yet to be demonstrated. Third, among its other drawbacks, the rule impairs significantly the search for truth in criminal justice. Finally, alternative methods for deterring and redressing fourth amendment violations exist or could be created, and those alternatives would be more effective and less costly than the exclusionary rule. . . .

Arguments Against the Exclusionary Rule

There are a number of arguments against the exclusionary rule. Several go to its effect on the "integrity" of the criminal justice system. Others question its deterrent value. Finally, there are arguments concerning its harmful effects, and suggestions that there are constitutionally and socially acceptable alternatives.

1. *The Exclusionary Rule Releases Dangerous Criminals, Encourages Plea Bargains, and Discourages Prosecution.* The most obvious objection to the exclusionary rule is that it prevents the conviction of criminals. At one level there are the notorious cases in which those guilty of serious crimes are released because essential evidence is suppressed. The overall impact on convictions is less clear. While it is difficult to quantify the number of convictions lost, several studies suggest the total is not insignificant.

A 1982 National Institute of Justice study of the effects of the exclusionary rule in California found a significant impact on the rate of conviction. According to the study, 4.8% of over 4,000 felony cases rejected for prosecution were declined by prosecutors because of search and seizure problems. The effect of the exclusionary rule on drug cases was even more pronounced. Approximately 30% of all felony drug cases were declined by prosecutors because of search and seizure problems. . . .

There is some consensus that the exclusionary rule "costs" the state only a small percentage of the total of all possible felony prosecutions, but this does not answer the question of what constitutes a "significant impact." A small percentage of all such cases is a very substantial number in absolute terms. Losing that many convictions certainly poses serious dangers to the community, and there is evidence that the number of lost convictions is concentrated particularly among certain crimes generally perceived as serious, e.g., weapons and drug offenses. Nor do percentages reflect the "cost" of public anger, and the heightened fear of crime, that may result from the release or truncated prosecution of serious criminals even in a small number of cases.

Searching for Evidence

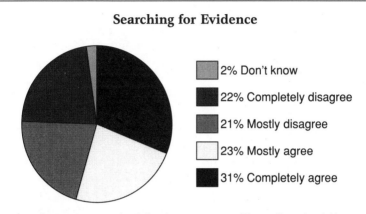

2% Don't know

22% Completely disagree

21% Mostly disagree

23% Mostly agree

31% Completely agree

In response to the following statement: The police should be allowed to search the houses of known drug dealers without a court order.

Source: Gallup Organization, May 1988.

The loss of evidence at trial is not the only price the state pays for continuation of the exclusionary rule. The rule may distort the criminal justice system by tipping the balance in favor of the accused. Prosecutors who anticipate losing cases at trial on "technicalities," or who find police conduct in given cases to fall within a "gray area," may be willing to trade reduced charges for a guilty plea. Or they may simply choose not to go forward in cases where there is a significant chance that essential evidence will be excluded.

The Breakdown of the System

2. *The Exclusionary Rule Excludes the Most Reliable Evidence and Undermines the "Truth-seeking" Function of the Criminal Justice Process.* A particular problem with the exclusionary rule is that it often excludes the most credible evidence of crime, namely

physical evidence within the possession or control of the defendant. In the words of the former Director of the Department's Bureau of Justice Statistics, Steven R. Schlesinger, the exclusionary rule is

> qualitatively different from other types of exclusion such as suppression of unreliable confessions, line-up evidence, or eyewitness identification, for in these areas suppression takes place because of specific doubts as to the reliability of the evidence.

The exclusionary rule thus interferes with the truth-finding function of the law in a way that other rules governing suppression, which concern the credibility of evidence, do not.

3. *The Exclusionary Rule Diminishes Respect for the Entire System of Justice.* To the extent that the preservation of the integrity of the courts and the criminal justice system as a whole is a fundamental purpose of suppression of reliable evidence, the exclusionary rule may actually work against it. Studies indicate that there is a widespread public perception that criminals are allowed to get off through "loopholes" and "technicalities," and that the courts are to blame. Public respect for the courts and for the criminal justice system suffers as a result of this departure from the truth-seeking function.

4. *The Exclusionary Rule Provides No Remedy for the Innocent.* In one sense, the exclusionary rule vindicates only the rights of criminals, i.e., persons who otherwise would probably be convicted. While the fourth amendment's protections against unreasonable searches and seizures belong to all, the exclusionary rule provides relief only to those persons accused of a crime from whom contraband or other incriminating evidence is obtained. People whose rights of privacy are violated, but who are not prosecuted, are afforded no remedy by the exclusionary rule. The exclusionary rule thus operates differently from enforcement mechanisms for other constitutional provisions, such as the right to jury trial or the assistance of counsel, which are concerned with the truth-finding function of the law and thereby protect the innocent as well as the guilty.

Misplaced Emphasis

5. *The Exclusionary Rule May Not Significantly Deter Police Misconduct.* At the heart of the current debate over the exclusionary rule is the issue of whether it does in fact deter police misconduct. . . .

One of the most prominent attacks on the deterrent value of the exclusionary rule has been mounted by Professor Dallin Oaks. Oaks believes that the rule acts neither as an effective special nor general deterrent.

With respect to special deterrence, Oaks and other commentators have observed that the exclusionary rule has a negligible deterrent effect on the transgressing officer because it does not punish him directly. Instead, the exclusion of evidence sanction is imposed most directly upon the prosecutor, who loses the ability to use the evidence in the case-in-chief against the accused. Moreover, delays in the criminal justice process and the lack of communication between prosecutors and arresting officers are such that policemen often do not know that a "bust" was lost because of their failure to abide by fourth amendment requirements. Many policemen believe that convictions are lost by prosecutors or judges for reasons unrelated to the exclusionary rule, and thus have no incentive to modify their behavior. Overall, Oaks suggests, the current system may tend to reward and punish police officers more on the basis of their performance in areas such as arrest and the seizure of evidence than on whether the fruits of their labors result in convictions. With respect to general deterrence, Oaks argues that the value systems of the police are not receptive to constitutional concerns. Moreover, the ever-changing rules governing the fourth amendment are complex, and difficult for police to comprehend and follow. The fact that such rules may not be communicated clearly to police compounds the problem.

A Cop's Nightmare

The exclusionary rule has become the police officer's nightmare. The courts cranked out so many restrictions on police that the 1960s have been called the "criminal-law revolution." It wasn't enough to require a search warrant: the search also had to be limited to a narrowly specified crime, and the warrant had to list facts amounting to "probable cause" for arrest. If the police presented facts suggesting stolen television sets, for example, the warrant would not allow a search for drugs in a desk drawer. . . .

No other democracy protects the rights of criminals over society's right to peace and security—and no other democracy has anywhere near America's drug problem. It is no coincidence that our drug problem greatly worsened after *Mapp v. Ohio.* . . .

We are in the middle of a drug epidemic. We don't need protection from the cop on the beat—we need protection from criminals. And our police can't fight drugs if they are hamstrung by laws that defy common sense.

Charles Brandt, *The Los Angeles Daily Journal,* January 5, 1990.

The question of systematic deterrence was not addressed specifically by Oaks. However, there does seem to be little question that many police departments have modified their institutional practices as a result of *Mapp v. Ohio* and its progeny. Professional departments now provide training and education to officers to make them fully aware of warrant requirements and the prerequisites for a valid warrantless search. What is more difficult to determine is the extent to which such reforms have affected actual police behavior or the number of fourth amendment violations.

Ultimately, the deterrent value of the rule is a question for empirical examination. However, any comparison of deterrence is of limited value if it only compares the exclusionary rule to having no enforcement mechanism, and leaves out the possibility of achieving as much or more deterrence through the adoption of one of the alternatives to the exclusionary rule.

Lowering Standards

6. *The Exclusionary Rule May Encourage Police and Judicial Misconduct.* Several authorities have speculated that the exclusionary rule may work to encourage a variety of police and judicial misconduct. Officers who learn that their searches were improper only after the fact are encouraged to lie about the circumstances under which the evidence was obtained, even to the point of perjuring themselves, to save the evidence.

Moreover, fear of the exclusionary rule may encourage the police to employ a variety of tactics designed to combat crime which may violate the fourth amendment but which are not subject to the rule. Police may use harassing tactics—such as frequent raids, or repeated arrest and release—which take contraband off the streets and reduce certain criminal activities by imposing a high "cost" on participation in the criminal activity, but which stop short of employing the steps of the justice system at which the exclusionary rule would be invoked. The net effect may, therefore, be an increase in fourth amendment violations as police attempt to work around the rule.

Related to these problems, as well as to the problem of judicial tinkering with probable cause discussed below, is the problem of judges "looking the other way" on police and magistrate misconduct. Because the price of suppressing evidence is so high, some judges may be willing to accept outrageous police stories of how evidence was obtained, or ignore complaints about warrant defects or the conduct of investigations, to keep evidence in. If the courts were able to review and sanction police conduct, and assess the adequacy of warrants, in a forum distinct from the prosecution of the accused, they would probably be far more exacting in their review.

7. *The Exclusionary Rule May Undercut the Fourth Amendment by Encouraging Judges to Lower the Threshold of Probable Cause.* A number of commentators have argued that the exclusionary rule

encourages judges to lower the threshold of probable cause. Because judges are sensitive to the problem of allowing criminals to go free, they have an incentive to find that the basis for police action was sufficient. The quantum of evidence necessary to constitute probable cause falls ever lower as precedents accumulate. More searches may be conducted without a warrant, and the requirements for getting a warrant become less stringent. If there were an alternative to the exclusionary rule that penalized police misconduct, but that did not require evidence suppression, judges might be more willing to hold police to a higher standard of probable cause, and the interests of the fourth amendment might thereby be better served.

Protecting the Murderer

There is a rule of evidence, used in all federal and state Courts in America, that defies logic, makes no sense whatsoever, and causes hundreds of serious miscarriages of justice each year. Its technical name is the Exclusionary Rule.

This pernicious rule prohibits the admission of evidence at trial if the evidence has been obtained by a policeman or other peace officer as a result of "unreasonable search and seizure" in violation of the Fourth Amendment to the U.S. Constitution. . . .

The Exclusionary Rule has created an upside-down system of criminal justice which diverts the focus of the criminal prosecution from the guilt or innocence of the defendant to a trial of the police! . . .

The Exclusionary Rule holds, in effect, that it is better for a murderer to go free than for the State to take advantage of any illegal conduct on the part of its officers.

L. Thaxton Hanson, from a brochure published by the Americanism Educational League, 1976.

---

8. *The Continuation of the Exclusionary Rule Discourages the Search for Alternatives.* The existence of the exclusionary rule may discourage the development of superior alternatives. Although the Chief Justice and others have invited Congress and the states to develop other approaches, and have indicated that the Supreme Court might give up the exclusionary rule once effective alternatives were in place, the incentive for finding such replacements may be inhibited by the existence of the rule, as it gives the impression that the Supreme Court has preempted the field.

9. *The Exclusionary Rule Distorts the Allocation of Judicial and Criminal Justice Resources.* The cost in time and resources ex-

pended in considering and disposing of suppression motions may be considerable. One study found 34% of all court time in one Chicago narcotics court to be spent on hearing motions to suppress. In addition to the time of trial courts, there is the time spent by prosecutors screening cases for exclusionary rule problems and defending against suppression motions, and the time spent by appellate courts in reviewing suppression decisions on direct review and on collateral attack. Given the reality of necessarily limited judicial and criminal justice resources, the justice system might be better served—and fourth amendment rights better protected—by an alternative that examines and sanctions search and seizure violations outside the prosecutorial process.

To the Extent the Exclusionary Rule Is Not Constitutionally Required, There Is No Principled Basis for Its Application to the States. As discussed above, the Supreme Court's justification of the exclusionary rule has narrowed considerably. In *Mapp v. Ohio*, the Court described the rule as "constitutionally necessary." But other Supreme Court opinions have generally not held that exclusion is a constitutional command of the fourth amendment itself. Indeed, in *United States v. Calandra*, Justice Powell wrote for the Court that "the [exclusionary] rule is a judicially created remedy designed to safeguard fourth amendment rights generally through its deterrent effect, rather than a personal constitutional right of the party aggrieved.". . .

Let States Decide

The Supreme Court has never overtly asserted or defended the proposition that it possesses the authority to exclude evidence in a case in which the state court itself would not violate the Constitution by admitting it, and it is difficult to see what constitutional authority the Court could point to as the basis for the assumption of such power. . . .

In any event, because the Court considers the propriety of applying the exclusionary rule "in a particular case" to be "an issue separate from the question whether the Fourth Amendment rights of the party seeking to invoke the rule were violated by police conduct," two consequences seem to follow as a matter of logic: first, the current broad application of the rule is objectionable as an unprincipled interference with state courts by the federal judiciary; second, the rule should at a minimum be returned to its status prior to *Mapp*, i.e., as a limitation on federal but not state action.

"The exclusionary rule places no limitations on the actions of the police."

Excluding Illegally Seized Evidence Is Necessary

Special Committee on Criminal Justice in a Free Society

The Fourth Amendment protects people from unlawful searches and seizures by police or government officials. In the following report, the Special Committee on Criminal Justice in a Free Society found that excluding illegally seized evidence in criminal trials does not burden the criminal justice system. The committee found that the exclusionary rule helps police maintain professionalism in their jobs. In addition, the committee found that the exclusionary rule does not prevent prosecutors from obtaining convictions. The committee was formed by the Criminal Justice Section of the American Bar Association (ABA) and funded by the ABA to study the impact of constitutional rights on crime and crime control in the United States.

As you read, consider the following questions:

1. Why does the committee state the Fourth Amendment involves costs but does not impede criminal justice?
2. What contributes to public misperception that Fourth Amendment rights let criminals go free, according to the committee?
3. What is important for the public to understand about constitutional rights, according to the committee?

Reprinted with the permission of the American Bar Association from *Criminal Justice in Crisis*, 1988. This report has been prepared by the Special Committee on Criminal Justice in a Free Society of the American Bar Association Criminal Justice Section. It has not been approved by and does not necessarily represent the official position of the American Bar Association or its Criminal Justice Section.

Probably the most controversial constitutional limitation imposed upon police and prosecutors is the Fourth Amendment exclusionary rule, which requires courts to exclude otherwise admissible evidence against a criminal defendant when the evidence was obtained by an illegal search or seizure. Much of the controversy can be attributed to the widely held perception that the exclusionary rule seriously handicaps law enforcement, both on the street and in the courtroom.

The Committee was charged with assessing the validity of that perception. This assessment was made with the understanding that restraints on the police power to search and seize are imposed by the Fourth Amendment and that such circumscription is both essential and deliberate in a free society. Justice Potter Stewart eloquently described this point:

> The exclusionary rule places no limitations on the actions of the police. The fourth amendment does. The inevitable result of the Constitution's prohibition against unreasonable searches and seizures and its requirements that no warrant shall issue but upon probable cause is that police officers who obey its strictures will catch fewer criminals.

Necessarily, the enforcement of the Fourth Amendment involves costs; but as Justice Stewart stated, "[T]hat is the price the framers anticipated and were willing to pay to ensure the sanctity of the person, home, and property against unrestrained governmental power."

The evidence which the Committee gathered indicates that the exclusionary rule achieves a significant measure of police compliance with Fourth Amendment search and seizure restrictions. Moreover, it shows that the exclusionary rule has relatively little adverse impact on the criminal justice system and no discernible effect on the crime rate or law enforcement's ability to control crime.

The Impact of the Exclusionary Rule

Those who have studied the issue have concluded that it is difficult, if not impossible, to measure precisely either the deterrent effect of the exclusionary rule or its so-called "cost." To the extent that police officers and prosecutors have made adjustments in their training and procedures because of the exclusionary rule, it may be said that the exclusionary rule has had significant impact on police arrests and searches. Police recruits are now trained from the beginning of their careers on Fourth Amendment requirements. Coordination between the police and prosecutors on arrest and search issues, including legal assistance in the drafting of warrants, unheard of before the exclusionary rule, now occurs in a number of cities. Also, after *Mapp v. Ohio* (1961) made the exclusionary rule applicable to the states, the use of search warrants by state and local police increased substantially. It is reasonable to conclude that police departments have made these efforts to comply with the Fourth Amendment because of the exclusionary rule.

Chipping Away at the Exclusionary Rule

Nothing is more precious to the privilege of being an American than the protection of our freedom afforded by the Bill of Rights. There has been no greater threat in history to the foundation of our freedom than the current assault on certain provisions of the Bill of Rights, specifically the Fourth Amendment, by politicians, judges and lawyers. . . .

After the *Mapp* decision, the exclusionary rule enjoyed its heyday. The rule of law was fairly simple: if a search warrant was found to have been issued without probable cause, then the evidence seized pursuant to that warrant was rendered inadmissible. Warrantless searches were presumed to be in violation of the Fourth Amendment unless sufficient evidence of probable cause could be demonstrated to validate such a search. In the legal world, the exclusionary rule had never been stronger.

In American society however, the constitutional analysis of the Supreme Court moved out of sync with the political pendulum. The "sex, drugs and rock and roll" sixties became the "just say no" eighties. To be identified in public life as a liberal was to be made the political equivalent of pond scum. The exclusionary rule changed from being referred to as the natural extension of the Fourth Amendment to a legal technicality used by lawyers and judges to release massive numbers of dangerous criminals onto the streets.

Paul A. Catalano, *Los Angeles Lawyer*, December 1991.

What then is the "cost" of the rule? To be sure the Committee heard complaints that the body of law defining Fourth Amendment restrictions is complex, and as a result, teaching, understanding, and obeying the Fourth Amendment can be both difficult and at times, frustrating for police departments. However, the witnesses testifying before the Committee certainly do not view the rule as an impediment to effective crime control. One police officer told our Reporter that in his experience, the Fourth Amendment was not a problem, as long as he was careful to keep his actions "within the guidelines." Similarly, an assistant chief of police told our Reporter: "I don't think the Constitution itself or the Bill of Rights . . . either are a major problem as far as law enforcement is concerned. . . . The price

91

of freedom is that you're going to have to guarantee rights—to be taken advantage of by criminals as well as the good people too." This viewpoint was echoed throughout the Committee's hearings.

Q. The public has the view that the system is not working because of the exclusionary rule. Is this a correct impression?

A. No, it isn't.

(Prosecutor)

Q. Do you agree that there's a broad public perception [that] court decisions [on] constitutional rights are one of the leading causes of crime?

A. It's the public perception.

Q. [Is that a valid perception?]

A. [I don't think so] . . . I think the leading cause of crime is poverty.

(Trial Judge)

Q. Do you agree with the perception that constitutional rights are a leading cause of crime?

A. I don't.

(Assistant Prosecutor)

The conclusion that the exclusionary rule neither causes serious malfunctioning of the criminal justice system nor promotes crime is strongly supported by practically all of our other witnesses and by our telephone survey respondents. Taken as a whole, the testimony and the survey results demonstrate that constitutional limitations are not seen as a relatively significant problem by the people who must work within those limitations.

Coping with Restrictions

The telephone survey respondents were asked several questions relating to the Fourth Amendment. They were asked to identify the factors that either interfered with their own job effectiveness or the effectiveness of the criminal justice system in general. In both instances, the courts' constitutional rulings were considered a relatively insignificant factor. The mean (average) score for police respondents bordered on the designation "disagree" in the survey concerning the proposition that "search and seizure restrictions routinely prevent police from detecting and solving crimes" or that such limitations "routinely result in prosecutorial refusal to accept cases or plea bargain."

It is especially worthy of note that the police, toward whom the deterrent force of the exclusionary rule is primarily directed, do not consider search and seizure proscriptions to be a serious obstacle. Prosecutors, also, do not believe such restrictions are a "routine" concern.

Other responses were more predictable. Defense lawyers voiced strong disagreement with the proposition that the police and prosecutors are routinely hampered by the exclusionary rule. Judges also disagreed with these propositions.

A More Professional Police Force

One 1982 survey by the government's National Institute of Justice warned that a large number of felonies were being thrown out of California courts because evidence was obtained in illegal searches. But later interpretations of the same data debunked this claim, proving that only a tiny percentage of cases were lost because of the rule. Says James Fyfe, "There is not one study that shows it affects more than 1.5 percent of all cases." Even in narcotics cases, where the impact is greatest, Peter Nardulli and others find that the rule has forced police to conduct searches more carefully. Says Richard Uviller, "They have learned to stop and think before they search—exactly what the Fourth Amendment wants them to do."

By far the most striking findings suggest that cops are proud of the way the reforms have shaped up their departments. In 1987 law student Myron Orfield interviewed members of a Chicago narcotics squad and found that all opposed eliminating the exclusionary rule. "It makes the police department more professional," said one. Without it, said another, an investigating policeman "would be like a criminal released in the midst of society."

Tamar Jacoby, *Newsweek*, July 18, 1988.

The testimony and the other survey results explain these answers. Police witnesses indicated that they have learned to cope with the restrictions placed upon them under the Fourth Amendment:

Q. To what extent are search and seizure rules a problem for you day to day?

A. I don't believe that they are a major problem. . . . We have an outstanding educational program on current search and seizure laws. Most of the officers are aware of them. Frankly, I don't think that it presents a big problem to us.

(Police Lieutenant) . . .

Q. [Do y]ou think it happens a lot that evidence is excluded because of a bad search?

A. Much less now than it was ten or twelve years ago. [M]ost

93

of the officers I see, take that extra effort to make sure the case is handled as best they can. . . . [T]hey have had to learn over the years . . . through their own mistakes . . . until they eventually saw what had to be done. . . .

(Police Lieutenant)

The Committee interviewed three chief prosecutors from different cities and one high ranking assistant from a large office in another city. One of these prosecutors, testifying as the designated representative of the National District Attorneys Association, noted that prosecutors identify drugs, sentencing, and various aspects of federal-state coordination as the major national issues, rather than the Fourth Amendment as currently interpreted.

Declining Cases

Three of the four prosecutors interviewed also believe the number of cases affected by the exclusionary rule has been declining in recent years:

[I]f you look at the numbers and you say how many times is the exclusionary rule responsible for cases being canned, I think the numbers are probably going down.

(Prosecutor)

Q. Do you have any estimate of the percentage of cases where [motions to suppress] are litigated and motions are granted?

A. It is very small. I don't have any.

(Prosecutor) . . .

To assess the wider significance of the testimony, the Committee wanted to know how many cases were being "lost" nationally because of the exclusionary rule. There are empirical studies conducted over the years which attempt to evaluate the costs of the rule and its impact on the criminal justice system. Although there is some disagreement, the weight of this authority is consistent with the Committee's evidence and establishes that the cases primarily affected by the rule are drug cases. Violent crime cases rarely are lost because of the rule, and the percentage of the total number of cases in the system that are lost because of the rule is relatively small. A comprehensive survey, published in 1983, of the studies which have been conducted on how the exclusionary rule has affected the filing of cases found that the number of cases lost is small:

• Overall in jurisdictions with prosecutorial screening between 0.2% and 0.6% to 0.8% of adult felony arrests are screened out because of illegal searches.

• Adding together data on each of the stages of felony processing (police releases, prosecutor screening, and court dismissals), we find that the cumulative loss resulting from illegal searches is in the range of 0.6% and 0.8% to 2.35% of all adult felony arrests.

• In felony arrests for offenses other than drugs or weapons possession, including violent crime arrests, the effects of the rule are lower; prosecutors screen out less than 0.3% of these felony arrests because of illegal searches, and the cumulative loss is no more than 0.3% to 0.7% of such arrests.

• Prosecutors screen out 2.4% of felony drug arrests (nowhere near the 30% claim of the National Institute of Justice), while the cumulative loss for drug arrests is probably in the range of 2.8% to 6% or 7.1%. (Weapons possession arrests may have a cumulative loss of about 3.4%, but data are very limited.)

• Very few arrests are lost by acquittals at trial following suppression of evidence.

The most striking feature of the data is the concentration of illegal searches in drug arrests (and possibly weapons possession arrests) and the extremely small effect on the arrests for other offenses, including violent crimes. . . .

The only exception to this conclusion found by the Committee, particularly in one major city, was in the enforcement of gun and drug laws. A prosecutor in that city, who agreed that generally, Fourth Amendment limitations were not a problem, noted that because of search and seizure issues, he refuses to prosecute 50% of the gun and drug arrests in his jurisdiction. Of those he does approve, between 80% and 85% survive motions to suppress. When asked if guns and drugs formed a special category of cases, he replied:

[Y]es. . . . We don't have Fourth Amendment problems in other areas. We haven't had a murder weapon suppressed in forty years, . . . or a bloody towel, or anything like that. It's just guns and drugs we found we have a hard time with.

This prosecutor added that most of these cases involved automobile stops, and notwithstanding the numbers, he did not think the Fourth Amendment was an obstacle:

Q. [Why are there so many cases rejected? Is the law unclear or are the police not following the law and then not telling you the true circumstances?]

A. I'd say it's more the latter; I think it boils down to the veracity of the officers, more often than not. . . . I think the appellate courts are going as far as they can to allow law enforcement to do their job. But if I took everything they brought to us, our system would be at a standstill. . . .

It bears reemphasis that, notwithstanding this problem, the overall number of cases lost or dismissed due to the exclusionary rule is extremely low. Research also demonstrates that far more cases are rejected or dropped for reasons other than the exclusionary rule.

The rule's impact, however, cannot be assessed simply through an examination of statistics. Prosecutors noted that even one arrest lost to the rule has a significant effect upon the public's perception of the value of the exclusionary rule. The media attention invariably focuses on such a case and creates the impression that the entire criminal justice system is functioning irrationally; that guilty, dangerous persons are routinely freed on technicalities. One witness described the impact of the public's image of the criminal system:

> So it is true that in a determinative sense it may be one case, but the effect of the single case on the public's perception of the criminal justice system and their support and willingness to vote bond issues to build a prison, et cetera, I think, are affected by single cases.

> (Prosecutor)

Other witnesses agreed that the publicity the rule receives fosters the public's belief that the system does not work. This problem is very troubling, but it is not a problem with the rule itself or one peculiar to it. Rather, it is one of many misperceptions regarding the criminal justice system and crime that need to be corrected.

Some judges and prosecutors told the Committee that even

The Test for a Democracy

The U.S. Supreme Court continues to make the gritty decisions that convert ideas into a way of life.

The court affirmed a principle known as the exclusionary rule, which requires that illegally obtained evidence be excluded from criminal trials.

For 75 years, the court has said society has more to fear from police misconduct than the consequences of letting a guilty person go free. . . .

Justice William Brennan said that while arriving at the truth is important, the suppression of valid but illegal evidence is necessary to protect our constitutional rights:

"So long as we are committed to protecting people from the disregard of their constitutional rights . . . inadmissibility of illegally obtained evidence must remain the rule, not the exception," Brennan wrote for the 5-4 majority.

Living up to tough rules is the test of a true democracy.

The Los Angeles Daily Journal, January 18, 1990.

---

though very few motions to suppress are granted, the litigation of such motions is time consuming. This criticism was sporadic and may reflect a more general problem in some cities of carrying a heavy caseload. This situation suggests that the source of the problem is overtaxed court systems. Moreover, it is to be expected that litigation conducted in accordance with constitutional safeguards will take more time than litigation not so conducted. More significant was the view of witnesses that the exclusionary rule enhanced the professionalism of police departments.

> Essentially, I really think that the Fourth Amendment and Fifth Amendment have really made the police officer better police officers because they have to be . . . smarter police officers. If you recall, in the 60's when the Johnson Commission reports came out, on the whole the police officers were underpaid and not much education was required. Now, in this state we have . . . a more professional corps of police officers who are brighter and better educated. I think, as we do away with these rights to protect defendants, I think it's ultimately [a] boomerang [effect].
>
> (Trial Judge)

After more than two decades with the exclusionary rule in place, the police have a considerable investment in the rule in its current form. They are not eager to replace it with different sanctions such as expanded civil remedies against the police officer or the department. Although the police expressed some objection to the notion of freeing guilty people because of a police officer's mistake, we were also told by one lieutenant that without the rule he feared there would be less reflection before police action, resulting in an increased number of civil suits against the police. . . .

It is essential that the public recognize that the exclusionary rule, despite its occasional complexity and the problems associated with that complexity, secures valuable rights and has little or no effect on the crime problem. This is not to say that Fourth Amendment issues are unimportant to society. If we, as a nation, want to maintain our right to privacy as guaranteed by the United States Constitution, it is critical that the public and the legal profession not be misled into believing that our constitutional rights contribute to the crime problem or work to hinder effective law enforcement. Precious constitutional rights should not be abrogated on the faulty premise that, without them, the crime problem will be solved or the failings of the criminal justice system will be corrected.

Distinguishing Between Fact and Opinion

This activity is designed to help develop the basic reading and thinking skill of distinguishing between fact and opinion. Consider the following statement: "The Fourth Amendment prohibits unreasonable searches and seizures." This is a factual statement. It can be checked by looking up the Bill of Rights in an encyclopedia and reading the Fourth Amendment. But the statement "The Fourth Amendment is not intended to protect the guilty" is an opinion. Many people believe that even those guilty of committing a crime should still be protected from unreasonable searches and seizures.

When investigating controversial issues, it is important that one be able to distinguish between statements of fact and statements of opinion. It is also important to recognize that not all statements of fact are true. They may appear to be true, but some are based on inaccurate or false information. For this activity, however, we are concerned with understanding the difference between those statements that appear to be factual and those that appear to be based primarily on opinion.

Most of the following statements are taken from the viewpoints in this chapter. Consider each statement carefully. *Mark O for any statement you believe is an opinion or interpretation of facts. Mark F for any statement you believe is a fact. Mark I for any statement you believe is impossible to judge.*

If you are doing this activity as a member of a class or group, compare your answers with those of other class or group members. Be able to defend your answers. You may discover that others come to different conclusions than you do. Listening to the reasons others present for their answers may give you valuable insights into distinguishing between fact and opinion.

O = opinion
F = fact
I = impossible to judge

1. The Supreme Court's decision in *Miranda v. Arizona* requires that arrestees be advised of their constitutional rights.

2. The right to remain silent reflects our unwillingness as a society to permit innocent people to incriminate themselves.

3. Remaining silent greatly reduces the chances of spending many years in prison.

4. The U.S. Supreme Court decided *Miranda v. Arizona* in June 1966.

5. *Miranda v. Arizona* was the Supreme Court's most important criminal case.

6. In the November 1987 issue of the *ABA Journal*, Stanford Law School's John Kaplan stated that arrested crime suspects confess just as easily when given their *Miranda* warning as when not given it.

7. After the Supreme Court reversed his conviction, Ernesto Miranda was again tried, convicted, and sentenced.

8. The Supreme Court made a grave misjudgment in the *Miranda* case.

9. The search and seizure exclusionary rule is subject to a number of well-founded criticisms.

10. The most obvious objection to the exclusionary rule is that it prevents the conviction of criminals.

11. A 1982 National Institute of Justice study of the effects of the exclusionary rule in California found that the rule decreased the rate of conviction.

12. The loss of evidence at trial is not the only price the state pays for continuation of the exclusionary rule.

13. The exclusionary rule interferes with the truth-finding function of the law.

14. Only the rights of criminals are vindicated by the exclusionary rule.

15. In *United States v. Calandra*, it was the majority opinion of the Supreme Court that the exclusionary rule was "designed to safeguard Fourth Amendment rights."

16. The most controversial constitutional limitation imposed upon police and prosecutors is the Fourth Amendment exclusionary rule.

17. After *Mapp v. Ohio* made the exclusionary rule applicable to the states, the use of search warrants by state and local police increased substantially.

18. *Gideon v. Wainwright* held that anyone accused of a felony for which a conviction might result in imprisonment is entitled to legal counsel at government expense.

Periodical Bibliography

The following articles have been selected to supplement the diverse views presented in this chapter.

Warren Burger — "Protecting Rights of the Convicted," *The Washington Times*, December 24, 1991. Available from 3600 New York Ave. NE, Washington, DC 20002.

Robert E. Burns — "Don't Make a Federal Case of Crime," *U.S. Catholic*, June 1991.

Thomas Fleming — "Law and/or Order," *Chronicles*, May 1992. Available from 934 N. Main St., Rockford, IL 61103.

John Wesley Hall — "The Fourth Amendment and the Exclusionary Rule Succumb After Long Illness," *The Arkansas Lawyer*, October 1991. Available from 400 W. Markham, Little Rock, AR 72201.

Fred E. Inbau — "*Miranda's* Immunization of Low Intelligence Offenders," *The Prosecutor*, Spring 1991. Available from National District Attorneys Association, 1033 N. Fairfax St., Suite 200, Alexandria, VA 22314.

Nicholas Katzenbach — "Justice—A Reality or an Illusion," *Pace Law Review*, Spring 1990. Available from William S. Hein & Co., 1285 Main St., Buffalo, NY 14209.

James J. Kilpatrick — "System Cares More for the Criminal's Rights," *Conservative Chronicle*, January 2, 1991. Available from PO Box 11297, Des Moines, IA 50340-1297.

Michael Kinsley — "Inadmissible," *The New Republic*, May 6, 1991.

Jeremy M. Miller — "Miranda Protection Is No Longer Good Law," *The Los Angeles Daily Journal*, January 9, 1991. Available from 915 E. First St., Los Angeles, CA 90012.

National Review — "Law Breakers and Law Makers," April 15, 1991.

Reader's Digest — "Crime and Punishment USA," March 1992.

Utne Reader — "The Bill of Rights Has a Close Call," July/August 1991.

Should the Criminal Justice System Enforce Crime Victims' Rights?

Chapter Preface

In 1987, three-year-old Nicholas Christopher watched as Pervis Tyrone Payne stabbed Nicholas's mother and sister to death in Millington, Tennessee. Payne was convicted of the crimes and sentenced to death. During the sentencing hearing, Nicholas's grandmother gave a victim impact statement, testifying that the boy cried out for his mother and baby sister at night and did not understand why they did not come home. Those who evaluated the sentencing agreed that this poignant testimony contributed to the jury's decision to sentence Payne to death.

The grandmother's role in Payne's sentencing is considered a victory by victims' rights advocates. Traditionally, victims were left out of the criminal justice process. As a result, many victims of crime felt powerless and abandoned by the system. They watched as lawyers and judges protected the constitutional rights of the criminal but did nothing to address the pain the victim experienced. Consequently, many victims now demand the right to be included in the justice process. Reflecting what many victims feel, Roberta Roper, a victims' rights activist whose daughter was murdered in 1982, says that victims' "primary goal is not harsh punishment or money but to be involved." Procedures like victim impact statements give victims a sense that they are participating in the justice process.

While critics of victims' rights may agree that victims deserve the sympathy and help of society, they do not agree that the criminal justice system is the right venue for recompensing victims. Such critics argue that the goal of the criminal justice system is to convict the criminal. In this view, the state represents the victim when it investigates the crime, brings the charges, takes the accused to trial, and incarcerates the defendant, if convicted. As Alan Dershowitz, a legal scholar, points out, "In using its power to punish the defendant, the government is on the side of the victim." Dershowitz and others contend that victims' rights are unnecessary. These critics conclude that victims should seek assistance not from the criminal justice system but from other governmental agencies.

Most Americans would agree that victims need more assistance and support from society. Whether the criminal justice system is responsible for providing this assistance is debatable. The viewpoints in this chapter debate the role of victims in the criminal justice system.

"Victims have no rights at all—merely privileges to be granted or withheld at the whim of criminal justice insiders."

Victims' Rights Must Be Expanded

Deborah Kelly

Victims' rights groups have gained legislative reforms for victims of crime. These reforms, though, have not helped victims, Deborah Kelly states in the following viewpoint. She contends that legislation designed to help victims has not been enforced by the criminal justice system. Kelly maintains that prosecutors in some cases do not inform victims that they have legal rights to participate in criminal proceedings. Kelly, the chair of the American Bar Association's Victims Committee, is an attorney with a Washington, D.C., law firm.

As you read, consider the following questions:

1. How does the criminal justice system fail to implement victim reforms, according to Kelly?
2. What does the author suggest that might further enforce victims' rights?
3. What are some of the other concerns of victims besides punishment, according to Kelly?

Although victims' reforms have become widespread over the last ten years, the idea still sends chills down the backs of many defense lawyers who think the principal focus of the victims' movement is how many days a defendant should be sentenced to the electric chair. Others believe that victims' reforms are paper promises adopted by legislators looking for a way to placate constituents worried about crime. . . .

Few Victims Notified

Clearly, many statutes have been passed in the name of crime victims. The question is, are they being delivered? The short answer is no. In fact, the mere existence of so many statutes may be misleading; in practice, most victims never benefit from these reforms.

Studies show that, in state after state, reforms on the books are little more than paper promises. Victim-impact statements are among the more widely known victims' reforms, yet preliminary studies suggest that most victims are either unaware of this right or do not use it. For example, in 1982 California bypassed the legislative process and enacted Proposition 8, the Victims' Bill of Rights. Designed to take control away from courthouse professionals and limit plea bargaining, this initiative allowed a victim "to attend all sentencing proceedings . . . and to reasonably express his or her views concerning the crime, the person responsible, and the need for restitution." A National Institute of Justice study, however, found that despite the fanfare that accompanied the passage of Proposition 8, less than 3% of eligible victims in California actually exercised their right to allocute.

Similarly, 33 states were studied in which probation officers are charged with the responsibility for preparing victim-impact statements. Results showed that only 18% of eligible victims attended sentencing and only 15% of eligible crime victims submitted written statements. Further, "where allocution is a statutory right, oral statements [were] presented by just over 9% of victims," most of whom are violent crime victims.

Undermining Victim Participation

These findings are reinforced in other states. In South Carolina, only 15% of those victims who were eligible actually presented victim-impact statements. This is hardly surprising, given that three-quarters of those victims who made it to the grand jury never even received notice of their opportunity to give a victim-impact statement. In Texas, the Crime Victims' Bill of Rights requires the Board of Pardon and Parole to notify victims about pending parole hearings. The only way the Board learns of victims' names and addresses is through the victim-impact statement that the prosecutor's office is supposed to submit. However, prosecutors seldom comply.

> [O]f the 5850 victim impact statements obtained by prosecution, only 106 (1.8%) were forwarded to the Board and of these 106, only six victims were notified by the Board about pending parole hearings. [Texas Crime Victims Clearinghouse, *Crime Victim Impact: A Report to the 70th Legislature* (1987).]

In addition to ignorance or disuse, many victims are not affected by criminal justice reforms because their case never reaches the state where such reforms are triggered. The initial charging decision determines whether any procedural rights will apply to victims, yet victims have no part in this decision. The effect of reforms on child victims, for example, is minimized because up to 90% of child abuse cases are not prosecuted. As the Supreme Court put it, "a private citizen lacks a judicially cognizable interest in the prosecution or non-prosecution of another." Of every 100 adult arrests for a felony, only three lead to trial; consequently there is no separate sentencing hearing. Assuming a minimum of one victim for each arrest, for 97 out of 100 felony victims, rights to allocute or present victim-impact statements are irrelevant in practice.

Indifference to Victims' Needs

For all its success, the victims-rights movement continues to face the indifference of many authorities to its demands. "Many officials believe that it is just too time-consuming and cumbersome to involve victims in such decisions as pretrial release and sentencing," says Jane Burnley, chief of the U.S. Office for Victims of Crime. One result is that most victims are unaware of their rights to participate. In 1982, Californians voted a constitutional amendment giving victims the right to address judges at their assailants' sentencing. Mostly because of ignorance, 97 percent failed to appear. Those who did speak in court had little effect on the sentencing outcome.

Ted Gest, Pamela Ellis-Simons, Anne Moncreiff Arrarte, and Scott Minerbrook, *U.S. News & World Report*, July 31, 1989.

Doing away with plea bargaining is not the way to implement victims' reforms. Not all victims want to go through the public ordeal of trial. Moreover, under the Constitution, the right to a public trial clearly belongs to the defendant, not the victim. California's experience with Proposition 8 illustrates that because plea bargaining benefits prosecutors, defense attorneys, and judges, it won't go away anyway. Although Proposition 8 banned plea bargaining after indictment or information in seri-

ous felonies, studies showed that its effect was to shift plea bargaining to earlier stages, and to dispose of felony cases so
quickly that victims were deprived of their statutory right to
speak in court. As a result, the very goals the initiative sought to
promote were arguably undermined.

The Legal Debate

As research pours in showing that victims are reaching a fraction of their intended audience, the Supreme Court has weighed
in to reinstitute the use of victim-impact testimony in capital
cases. In *Payne v. Tennessee* [1991], the Court overturned both
Booth v. Maryland [1987] and *South Carolina v. Gathers* [1989]. In
those prior cases, the Court had ruled that it was unconstitutional to introduce victim-impact testimony to a jury at the sentencing stage of a capital trial. The majority's reasoning was that
the effect of the crime on the deceased victim's family had
nothing to do with the defendant's "blameworthiness."

The passionate dissent of O'Connor, Rehnquist, and Kennedy
in *Gathers* had signaled that *Booth v. Maryland* [1987] was far
from settled precedent. As Justice O'Connor wrote:

> Just as Gathers' own background was important to the jury's
> assessment of him as a 'uniquely individual human bein[g]'
> . . . so information about his equally unique victim was rele-
> vant to the jury's assessment of the harm he had caused and
> the appropriate penalty. Nothing in the Eighth Amendment
> precludes the community from considering its loss in assess-
> ing punishment nor requires that the victim remain a faceless
> stranger at the penalty phase of a capital trial.

In *Payne* the Court seized the opportunity to turn the *Gathers*
dissent into law. Payne was convicted of repeatedly stabbing a
young mother, her two-and-a-half-year-old daughter, and her
four-year-old son with a butcher knife. Only the little boy survived and at trial, the victim's grandmother testified that he still
cries out for his mother and his sister. Against a *Booth* challenge, the appellate court held that the prosecutor's introduction
of these statements was either relevant to show the savagery of
the attack or harmless error given the overwhelming evidence
of guilt.

As the Circuit Court wrote,

> It is an affront to the civilized members of the human race to
> say that at sentencing in a capital case, a parade of witnesses
> may praise the background, character and good deeds of
> Defendant (as was done in this case), without limitation as to
> relevancy, but nothing may be said that bears upon the char-
> acter of, or the harm imposed upon, the victims.

The Supreme Court in *Payne* reiterated Justice Scalia's dissent
in *Booth* that the effect a crime has on the victim has always
been relevant to a defendant's "blameworthiness."

If a bank robber aims his gun at a guard, pulls the trigger, and kills his target, he may be put to death. If the gun unexpectedly misfires he may not. His moral guilt in both instances is identical, but his responsibility in the former is greater.

The Court also rejected its previous conclusion in *Booth* that victim-impact testimony could skew sentencing decisions in favor of articulate, high-status victims and their families. The Court noted that in *Gathers*, evidence was introduced concerning a victim who was "an out of work, mentally handicapped individual, perhaps not, in the eyes of most, a significant contributor to society, but nonetheless a murdered human being."

More Victims of Crime

More than 35 million people were victims of some kind of personal crime, household crime, or vehicle theft in 1991, says the Bureau of Justice Statistics. The report is based on a survey of 95,000 people in 48,000 households. Included: 22 million crimes that weren't reported to police.

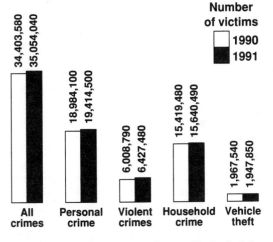

Source: National Crime Victimization Survey; Bureau of Justice Statistics.

Although the Supreme Court affirmed that defendants must be treated as "uniquely individual human beings," it found that this did not preclude admitting testimony which showed that victims were also unique human beings. The Court underscored that defendants are given virtually limitless options to introduce mitigating evidence at sentencing. Victim-impact testimony offers "a glimpse of the life which the defendant chose to extinguish." The *Payne* majority characterized victim-impact testimony as merely providing a relevant balance of the "human costs of the crime of which the defendant stands convicted." Fairness toward defendants, the Court concluded, does not preclude consideration of victims. As the Court affirmed, "[j]ustice, though due to the accused, is due to the accuser also. The concept of fairness must not be strained till it is narrowed to a filament. We are to keep the balance true."

Although the Supreme Court has characterized its reopening the doors to victims' participation at sentencing as a balancing of interests, many attorneys remain convinced that any gain for victims must be a loss for defendants. While this sentiment drives opposition to victims' reforms, it is ultimately misguided.

Does Not Slow Down System

Empirical studies suggest that victim participation does not lead to harsh sentences. Cases where defendants and victims know each other routinely result in lesser sentences than when victims and offenders are strangers. A study by New York's Victim Service Agency found that crime victims were more likely to be consulted by prosecutors when they had a prior relationship with the offender, and when consulted, those victims' recommendations usually lead to "softer dispositions." Courts routinely sentence those who victimize family members less seriously than those who victimize strangers. For example, convicted child sex abusers receive less time than offenders who sexually abuse adults, in large part because most child abusers know their victims.

There is virtually no evidence that the victims' participation is at the defendant's expense. A national study of 36 states, for example, found that to the extent that victim-impact statutes had an effect on defendants it was to enforce restitution orders; the effect on sentence type and length was negligible. Further, judges interviewed in states with victims' rights legislation indicated that the legislation did not tip the balance in favor of victims.

A national study of victim participation in plea negotiations concluded that, contrary to what prosecutors originally envisioned, victims did not slow down the process or demand stiff sentences but instead, usually agreed to prosecutors' recommendations. A similar, more recent study of victim participation in plea bargaining confirmed this finding and concluded that such involvement helped victims "without any significant detrimental impact to the interests of prosecutors and defendants."

This should not be surprising because victims' reforms were designed not to hurt defendants, but to help victims. The evidence is that, however underutilized, the reforms accomplish that purpose. A national study in states with victims' reforms concluded that victim satisfaction with prosecutors and the criminal justice system was increased without infringing on the defendants' rights. Victims who perceived themselves to be included or consulted in decision-making were more satisfied with the criminal justice system and more willing to cooperate with prosecutors in the future than those who were not informed or consulted. Other studies have confirmed that victims' satisfaction with the criminal justice system depends more on how they were treated than whether or not the defendant was severely punished.

What About the Victim?

Once a criminal case enters the judicial system, the government takes the place of the injured party. The victim becomes a witness, at most, and has no legal standing.

Victims and their families can be excluded from courtroom proceedings, and prosecutors are under no obligation to contact them before arranging plea bargains.

Even when laws are passed to grant victims more rights—like the Virginia, Maryland and District statutes that allow submission of victim impact statements to the court—they have no legal recourse if those laws aren't followed.

By contrast, a criminal defendant's right to be present at trial and to be kept informed is protected under the Constitution.

"Defendants are guaranteed rights," said Joyce Williams, director of the Fairfax County Victim Witness Assistance Program. "We want their rights to be protected, but what about victims of crime?"

Melanie Howard, *The Washington Times*, November 10, 1991.

The impact of victims' reforms makes it clear that much of the *us* versus *them* rhetoric stirred up by the mere mention of victims' issues is hyperbole. Can victims' advocates simultaneously be committed civil libertarians? Of course; compassion for victims does not preclude concern for defendants' rights. In fact, those people disproportionately trapped by violent crime are the lower income members of minority groups that civil libertarians care about and who would attain a greater voice through the increased use of victims' statutes.

The solution to victims' concerns is not to throw all defendants in jail for two lifetimes. This would not only be unjust toward defendants, it would have little effect on victims because for most victims there is no defendant. The offender is not arrested or the case is not prosecuted. Punishing the defendant is not synonymous with helping the victim. To say that victims only want vengeance is to cheapen their needs and understate the trauma that crime inflicts. Although the outcome of a case is clearly important to them, at best it is only one of many concerns. Some of the most pressing and unaddressed needs of victims, such as money and improved security, have nothing to do with the criminal justice system. Within the criminal justice system, study after study has shown that victims' satisfaction with it depends more on how they were treated than how severely their assailants were punished.

Although victims' reforms in some cases may make life more challenging for defense attorneys, this is not equivalent to an attack on the Constitution. Victims' reforms reflect the consensus of most states that the interests of the 35 million people who are victims of crime annually should factor into the criminal justice system. Victims' reforms also reflect an effort to interject compassion into a system that often equates defending the accused with destroying the victim.

Despite the impressive count of statutes, it is clear that the integrity of victims' reforms is threatened because at present most "victims' statutes" are little more than paper promises. In many instances those charged with notifying victims of their rights, do not. Ironically, the greatest resistance to correcting this and putting teeth in victims' reforms may come from prosecutors, who are concerned that their turf will be invaded and their ability to dispose of cases will be slowed considerably. Proposals to provide victims with a cause of action if they are not notified of their rights run the risk of causing this fragile alliance between prosecutors and victims' groups to disintegrate entirely.

Some victims' rights statutes, however, cry out for implementation if not reform. Compelling evidence exists that victims' reforms are at best honored in the breach. In spite of the quantity of statutes described above, if there is any truth to the adage that there is no right without a remedy, in the final analysis victims have no rights at all—merely privileges to be granted or withheld at the whim of criminal justice insiders.

"The laudable strides made on behalf of the victims of crime have begun to run roughshod over those suspected and convicted of crimes."

Victims' Rights Must Be Curbed

James R. Acker

The criminal justice system has made positive gains by support-ing victims' rights, but some of these gains have been at the cost of defendants' rights, according to James R. Acker. In the follow-ing viewpoint, Acker contends that victims' rights should not be so broad that they threaten important constitutional safeguards that protect defendants. Acker is an assistant professor at the School of Criminal Justice at the State University of New York in Albany.

As you read, consider the following questions:

1. What are four attempts by the criminal justice system to address the needs of crime victims, according to Acker?
2. What are four rights used by defendants that are in danger of being taken away, according to the author?
3. What evidence does Acker use to support his claim that public sentiment is antidefendant?

From James R. Acker, "Social Sciences and the Criminal Law: Victims of Crime—Plight vs. Rights." Reprinted with permission from the *Criminal Law Bulletin* 28 (1), © 1992 Research Institute of America, Inc., Warren Gorham Lamont Professional Publishing Division, 210 South St., Boston, MA 02111. All rights reserved.

In the wake of crime, many crime victims and their intimates begin to perceive themselves and the world around them in distressingly different terms. They may feel helpless, insecure, and threatened by what they once considered a safe and protective environment. People whose lives have been rocked by crime sometimes relinquish their belief in a just world, can become distrustful and incapable of sharing intimacy with others, and often suffer other ill effects. In addition, many Americans are held hostage by the fear of crime. Such fears sometimes almost literally render some people prisoners in their own homes, forcing them to curtail drastically their normal life activities. . . .

Societal responses to crime have taken different forms. On the one hand, a number of measures have been implemented to assist the victims of crime and otherwise to promote crime victims' interests. At the same time, many "get tough" measures against suspected and convicted criminal offenders have been proposed and enacted. Ironically, the social backlash against crime in some respects has blurred the distinction between victim and criminal.

Gains in Victims' Rights

Victim-directed measures. Little more than a decade ago, it was not uncommon for victims of crime to be ignored, mistreated, and even "revictimized" during their interactions with the criminal justice system. Since then, official attitudes and actions toward crime victims have changed dramatically. Indeed, proponents of victims' "rights" have exalted that the innocent who bear the brunt of crime are "no longer the 'forgotten victim,'" [according to Roland in "Progress in the Victim Reform Movement: No Longer the 'Forgotten Victim,'" in the *Pepperdine Law Review*, 1989].

Financial restitution is one form of assistance that has increasingly been provided. Restitution is the court-ordered payment of money or services by an offender to the victim of a crime. This payment is often required as a condition of probation or parole. Victim restitution is hardly new to the criminal law; in fact, this form of compensation dates back centuries and was the normal redress for victims of wrongdoing before criminal prosecution became a public function. While all states authorize court-ordered restitution for crime victims, statutes in over half the states and under federal authority now require judges to order convicted offenders to make restitution to their victims, or else to make written findings justifying why restitution should not be paid.

For several reasons, including offenders' indigency, difficulties with enforcement, and because wrongdoers frequently are neither apprehended nor convicted, victim restitution orders have significant limitations. Victim compensation programs, however, also can help provide redress to victims of crime. Compensation differs from restitution in significant ways. Monetary payments are made from a government fund rather than directly from a convicted offender under compensation plans. Furthermore, compensation, unlike restitution, does not require the prior conviction of a criminal offender, and thus represents a more dependable source of financial assistance for many crime victims. The federal Victims of Crime Act of 1984 (VOCA) has spurred improvements in state victim compensation programs by establishing a Crime Victims Fund that provides for revenue sharing with qualifying states.

Although the compensation awards to crime victims have increased greatly in recent years and have become more widely available, many states' programs retain significant exclusions that deny full compensation to crime victims, or that prohibit recovery altogether for certain classes of offenses. Moreover, crime victims usually cannot receive compensation for all of their crime-related losses. For example, while the laws in many states protect crime victims against employment discharge for necessary court appearances, most states do not require compensation for lost wages due to related work absences. To help supplement their victim compensation revenues, and for equitable reasons, many states have enacted "Son of Sam" laws, which divert offenders' crime-related profits into compensation funds and victim restitution payments.

Many other legal measures have been implemented that provide no direct redress to victims of crime, but that nevertheless are designed to promote victims' interests in the criminal justice system. Crime victims have widely reported being disaffected by their interactions with police, prosecutors, and judicial personnel. Victims often perceive officials as treating them like insignificant cogs in the wheels of justice, allowing them no input into decisions, giving them no notice of proceedings, nor even extending common courtesies as "their"cases are processed through the system. The measures taken in response to these concerns not only recognize the special interests of crime victims in the processing and disposition of criminal cases, but also make good business sense. Criminal justice officials must depend upon victim cooperation furthering their own interests.

Upholding Victims' Rights

Proposed constitutional amendments. The most ambitious efforts made on behalf of crime victims have been proposals to amend the federal Constitution to provide victims with enforceable legal rights. In 1982, the President's Task Force on Victims of Crime recommended that a supplemental protection be appended to the Sixth Amendment: "Likewise, the victim, in every criminal prosecution shall have the right to be present and to be heard at all critical stages of judicial proceedings." The Constitution of course remains without affirmative protections for crime victims, but numerous states, either statutorily or through state constitutional provisions, have enacted "Victims' Bills of Rights" that make such guarantees. The specifics of these enactments range from platitudinous affirmations that crime victims have a right to "be treated by agents of the state with dignity, respect and sensitivity during all phases of the criminal justice process," to more concrete provisions guaranteeing crime victims notice of and the right to participate in different case proceedings.

The Danger of Reforms

Victims of crime are a powerful force in the American criminal justice system. They are the key eyewitnesses who lead the police to a suspect. Prosecutors and judges depend on victims for their testimony in court. Once victimized, some individuals are unable to forget their experience and many become active lobbyists for much-needed criminal reform. However, there comes a point where these reforms, while expanding victims' rights, impinge on the rights of others. At that point, the energies and efforts funneled into reform can turn into a reprisal against the offender.

Dina R. Hellerstein, *American Criminal Law Review*, vol. 27, no. 2, 1989.

Victim impact statements. Among the more prominent types of victim-oriented measures is the widespread legislative authorization of the use of victim impact statements (VIS) for sentencing purposes in criminal cases. Usually prepared by a probation officer or another officer of the court a typical VIS contains information about the physical, financial, and psychological harm suffered by the crime victim and/or the victim's immediate family, and sometimes includes the opinions of those affected by the crime about an appropriate disposition for the offender. The VIS may be considered by the sentencing authority in criminal cases in at least forty-seven states and in the federal courts. Initially, the U.S. Supreme Court had forbidden the introduction of VISs in capital trials. It did so on the premise that victim characteristics and the harm suffered by a homicide victim's survivors are irrelevant to the offender's culpability and in the unique context of death penalty proceedings inject arbitrary considerations into the sentencing process. However, the Court has reversed itself on this issue, and recently approved the admission of victim impact evidence even in capital cases. Some have objected to the use of VISs in noncapital cases as well as capital ones, fearing that the sentencer is apt to be moved by sympathy for the victim's plight, and thus will be excessively punitive toward the offender. While a complete assessment of the impact of VISs upon sentencing judges remains to be made, preliminary evidence suggests that such fears might be exaggerated. In the first place, notwithstanding statutory authorization (or even requirement), judges are not always presented with crime victims' input prior to sentencing.

Moreover, when VISs *are* introduced, victims of crime typically are not as harsh or punitive in their views about offenders as might be anticipated. Additionally, judges' sentences do not seem to be influenced greatly by the contents of VISs. At the same time, crime victims who are given the opportunity to express themselves to the court through a VIS or through personal testimony often have more positive attitudes about the criminal justice system than do their counterparts who have not had these opportunities.

Much progress has been made in recent years in the laws and customs pertaining to victims of crime. Less than a decade ago Chief Justice Warren Earl Burger's opinion for the U.S. Supreme Court in *Morris v. Slappy* chastised a lower court because it had "wholly failed to take into account the interest of the victim in these crimes." The Chief Justice admonished generally that "in the administration of criminal justice, courts may not ignore the concerns of victims." Now, however, some observers are wondering if the pendulum has swung too far, and whether the laudable strides made on behalf of the victims of crime have begun to run roughshod over those suspected and convicted of crimes.

A Disturbing Trend

Offender-directed measures. Just as support for victims of crime has continued to grow in recent years, societal tolerance for acts of crime increasingly has waned. This mood of intolerance is reflected directly in public attitudes, as well as in the interpretation, application, and promulgation of laws affecting those suspected, accused, and convicted of crime. There is, of course, perfect consistency in being supportive of crime victims and being opposed to crime. The corollary, however, that being solicitous of the rights of the accused and restrained toward those convicted of crime somehow is to be "anti-victim," is a disturbing tenet that is implicit in some of the victims' rights rhetoric.

In 1989, 84 percent of the respondents to a Roper public opinion survey were of the opinion that the courts in their locale dealt "not harshly enough" with criminals. A Gallup poll conducted the same year revealed that 82 percent of the sample favored or strongly favored making it more difficult for inmates convicted of violent crimes to be paroled, and 68 percent favored or strongly favored prohibiting suspects accused of violent crimes from being released on bail while awaiting trial. Nearly one in five respondents supported allowing the police to search homes without a warrant. In response to the following question: "Which are you more worried about—that some criminals are being let off too easily, or that the constitutional rights of some people accused of committing a crime are not being upheld?"—70 percent of the sample were more concerned that criminals were let off too easily, compared to 16 percent who expressed more concern about abuses of constitutional rights.

Judges may not directly follow public opinion polls. Nevertheless, many state court judges are elected, and other state judges and the federal judiciary are appointed and confirmed by lawmakers who most certainly are responsive to public opinion. The courts have limited the constitutional protections of suspected and convicted criminals in a number of different areas. There have been significant legislative trends in this same direction.

For example, preventive detention statutes denying pretrial release to both suspected juvenile and adult offenders have been implemented and upheld by the courts. Police investigative powers have been enhanced by the U.S. Supreme Court's chipping away at *Miranda* rights, especially in the context of waiver of those rights and through the creation of a "public safety" exception to *Miranda*. The Fourth Amendment's probable cause requirement has been substantially denuded, and in many circumstances has been supplanted by murky balancing tests and elusive notions of reasonableness. The requirement for individualized suspicion of wrongdoing under the Fourth Amendment has completely evaporated in the face of such overriding governmental interests as employee drug-testing and drunk driving crackdowns. Simultaneously, the exclusionary rule has been whittled away and lambasted in judicial decisions, dispensed with entirely under the "good faith exception," and is a popular item for the chopping block in legislative crime bills.

Restricting Defendants' Rights

At trial, the destruction or disposal of potentially exculpatory evidence by agents of the state is not necessarily a constitutional violation. Face-to-face cross-examination must sometimes yield in the interest of protecting child witnesses. Involuntary confessions admitted into evidence at criminal trials can be overlooked under the harmless error rule.

Insanity tests have been restricted severely and the insanity defense has been eliminated altogether in some jurisdictions.

Defendants who succeed in pleading and being adjudged not guilty by reason of insanity might wish that they had not, for automatic civil commitment may follow and endure long beyond the maximum jail or prison sentence that could have been imposed upon conviction for the alleged crime. Verdicts of "guilty but mentally ill"—bastardized judgments that brand offenders as both bad and mad—exist in at least a dozen jurisdictions as an alternative disposition to ensnare defendants with the temerity to plead not guilty by reason of insanity.

Throwing the Legal System Off Balance

The Supreme Court put a powerful stamp of approval on victim impact statements—testimony from victims and family members relating the financial, physical and emotional effects of the crime on them. The high court ruled in *Payne vs. Tennessee* that juries could hear victim impact statements before sentencing offenders in death penalty cases.

But the *Payne* decision disturbed some legal experts, who say it is the harbinger of a trend toward unfairly restricting the rights of the accused.

The intent of the Constitution was to put the burden on the prosecution to prove guilt beyond a reasonable doubt, said William W. Greenhalgh, a professor at Georgetown University Law Center who specializes in criminal and constitutional law. Expanding victims' rights threatens to lessen that burden, he says, and throw the legal system off balance.

Melanie Howard, *The Washington Times*, November 10, 1991.

Convicted offenders are filling prisons in record numbers. Prison populations more than doubled during the 1980s. Nearly 330,000 adult offenders were incarcerated at year's end in 1980, compared to a staggering 710,000 at the end of 1989. The number of juveniles confined in public and private facilities likewise has swelled. Death rows across the country house an all-time high of over 2,400 condemned prisoners, while executions have occurred not only in such familiar places as Florida, Georgia, and Texas, but in Illinois, Oklahoma, Missouri, and other states outside of the Deep South.

Those who are behind prison walls find it increasingly difficult to have their convictions and sentences reviewed in the courts, because of a judicially created obstacle course of procedural forfeitures and cut-backs on federal habeas corpus. Prisoners may be exposed to mandatory life term sentences upon conviction for drug offenses and other nonhomicidal crimes, and increasingly may face "death by incarceration" under life-without-parole statutes that are in ef-- --- many jurisdictions. The time served by the incarcera--- ---ot to be easy time, in light of the badly overcrowded p-- --hich offenders are confined, and due to the U.S. Suprem-- --- sire neither to recognize or police legal rights for the oned. . . .

Maintaining Legal Boundaries

Criminal violence understandably is of concern to a great many Americans. The incidence and rates of violent crimes once again have begun to climb, and are skyrocketing to record heights. It is impossible not to be sympathetic to the plight of victims of crime. After years of seeming indifference, both the law and official actors in the criminal justice system have become more responsive to the concerns of crime victims.

However, the logical corollary of enhanced consideration for crime victims is not retrenchment of the rights that protect those suspected and convicted of crime, nor the reconfiguration of rules of law that govern substantive criminal offenses and the scope of defenses such as excuse or justification. To the contrary, the boundaries of the law must be maintained all the more firmly in the face of counterpressures stemming from the fear and anger about crime that are associated with victims' rights movements. Otherwise, constitutional safeguards and rational legal policies will regrettably be added to the swelling roster of victims of crime.

"The use of victim impact evidence . . . advances victims' interests only at a serious cost to capital defendants' Eighth Amendment rights."

Victims' Rights Threaten Defendants' Rights

Catherine Bendor

Victim impact evidence is testimony given by crime victims or their relatives concerning the harm they suffered from a defendant's actions. In the following argument, Catherine Bendor states that when victims or their families are allowed to speak at criminal sentencing hearings the court allows emotional rather than rational motives to influence sentencing. This is unfair and violates the Eighth Amendment's prohibition against cruel and unusual punishment, Bendor concludes. Bendor is with the legal department of Amnesty International in London, England.

As you read, consider the following questions:

1. What three reasons does the author give to show that *Payne v. Tennessee* is flawed?
2. What aspect of punishment is emphasized by victim impact statements? Why is this a bad idea, according to the author?
3. Why does Bendor say that balancing the victims' rights with the defendants' rights "contravenes" the sentencing procedures?

From Catherine Bendor, "Defendants' Wrongs and Victims' Rights: *Payne v. Tennessee,*" *Harvard Civil Rights Civil Liberties Review* 27 (Winter 1992): 219-43. Copyright © 1992 by the President and Fellows of Harvard College. Reprinted with permission.

Since the beginning of the modern era of death penalty jurisprudence marked by the United States Supreme Court's decision in *Furman v. Georgia* [1972], the Supreme Court has consistently championed the idea that capital punishment is both qualitatively and quantitatively different from other forms of punishment. Consequently, in order to guarantee that a sentence of death comports with the Eighth Amendment's prohibition against cruel and unusual punishment, the Supreme Court has established that capital defendants have a right to heightened procedural safeguards to ensure that a sentence of death is not imposed in an arbitrary or capricious manner. A decision to sentence a criminal defendant to death must be based on carefully reasoned deliberation rather than passion, prejudice or any other arbitrary factor.

Flawed Ruling

In *Payne v. Tennessee* [1991], the Supreme Court departed from its previous emphasis on stringent procedural protection for capital defendants and held that the Eighth Amendment does not bar capital sentencing juries from considering "victim impact" evidence—evidence describing the personal characteristics of the victim and the impact of the crime on the victim's family. *Payne* flatly overruled two decisions, *Booth v. Maryland* [1987] and *South Carolina v. Gathers* [1989], both of which held that the Eighth Amendment bars the introduction of victim impact evidence in capital sentencing proceedings because such evidence is irrelevant in determining the defendant's blameworthiness and poses an impermissible risk of unfair prejudice to the defendant. The *Payne* Court held that victim impact evidence merely informs the jury about the harm caused by the defendant's crime, a factor that has always been relevant in the criminal law. The majority further reasoned that admitting victim impact evidence provides a necessary means of balancing the interests of the victim and the defendant in capital sentencing trials. . . .

The majority's ruling in *Payne v. Tennessee* is flawed in several respects. First, the majority's broad conception of the harm caused by the defendant, which includes both the direct and indirect consequences of the defendant's act, does not comport with the traditionally accepted rationales for capital punishment underlying the Court's previous Eighth Amendment decisions. Second, the Court fails to specify the exact role to be played by victim impact evidence. The introduction of this powerful evidence is likely to lead the jury to base its decision on purely emotional reactions, or on an evaluation of the victim's social worth, neither of which have been acceptable bases for criminal sentencing decisions. The Court neither explains how it is possible to prevent these factors from becoming the bases for the jury's decision, nor provides any explanation of how victim impact evidence is otherwise relevant to the capital sentencing decision. Third, the Court's notion that the law should somehow provide an even balance between victims and defendants in sentencing proceedings is inconsistent with the basic purpose of sentencing—to determine the appropriate fate for the defendant, not the victim. . . .

The Harm of Victims' Rights

Increased concern for victims of crimes has developed within the justice system. The term "victims' rights" represents an appealing concept, acceptable to all and free from controversy. As one commentator cleverly asked: "Who could be anti-victim?" [according to Lynne Henderson in "The Wrongs of Victims' Rights," *Stanford Law Review*, 1985]. When one contemplates an individual who has been violated physically or destroyed financially by a crime, and who must then be confronted by an insensitive bureaucracy while reporting and testifying in connection with the criminal case, the answer to the question seems obvious: "No one." But while we may have compassion for the victims, there is an additional, important question: "What about the constitutional rights of the criminally accused?" This traditional concern of the justice system can be easily neglected when the focus shifts toward the victim.

Dina R. Hellerstein, *American Criminal Law Review*, vol. 27, no. 2, 1989.

The determination of how and to what extent the harm caused by a defendant's act should be considered in the sentencing process depends on the justification for which the punishment is being imposed. Of the four traditional rationales for criminal punishment—deterrence, retribution, incapacitation and rehabilitation—the only justification to which victim impact evidence directly relates is retribution. Retribution is a complex concept that encompasses two distinct considerations: the reason for imposing punishment, and the question of whose interests are to be vindicated through the punishment of an offender. With regard to the reason for imposing punishment, retribution has two discrete meanings. One view—that of "moral retribution"—focuses on the moral wrongness of the defendant's act and is based on the idea that an offender must pay a "debt" to society to make amends for his crime. A second concept of retribution is that of retaliation or revenge. This theory is premised on the notion that "society has a right to retaliate against those who have hurt it or failed to follow its rules, [according to Lynne N. Henderson in 'The Wrongs of Victims' Rights,' in the *Stanford Law Review*, 1985]."

An emphasis on the harm caused by an unlawful act in criminal sentencing does not comport with the moral retributionist basis for punishment, which is premised on punishing moral culpability and requires a focus on intent. The retaliation theory, however, focuses on the harm caused since its purpose is to avenge that harm. The introduction of victim impact evidence highlights the harm caused and thus furthers the purposes of retaliation.

The punishment-as-vengeance theory is problematic. In *Furman*, Justice Marshall decried the imposition of criminal penalties for vengeance alone, stressing that other aims have always been accepted as proper goals of punishment. As Marshall explained, the Eighth Amendment was adopted precisely to prevent punishment from becoming synonymous with vengeance: "If retribution alone could serve as a justification for any particular penalty, then all penalties selected by legislatures would by definition be acceptable means for designating society's moral approbation of a particular act." The retaliatory aspect of retribution has been widely condemned as an illegitimate purpose of the criminal law by judges, state legislators and social commentators.

In considering the question of whose interests are to be vindicated by the criminal justice system, it is important to note the distinction between using the system to achieve vengeance on behalf of society and using the system to satisfy the vengeful instincts of individual victims or family members. Private retaliation was the customary means of seeking redress for wrongs committed until the growth of the state. The increasing recognition of crime as a public wrong transformed redress into a public concern. Allowing the severity of punishment to satisfy the desire for vengeance of individual victims or their survivors violates the principles of proportionality and equality that underlie determinate sentencing. The Supreme Court has recognized the public nature of our criminal justice system and its rulings have aimed at maintaining it as such.

Morally Offensive

The *Payne* Court did not explicitly accept pure retaliation as a legitimate purpose of criminal punishment. Instead, the Court stressed that the harm caused by a criminal defendant has always been an important consideration in criminal punishment and is a relevant factor for the sentencer to evaluate. Chief Justice Rehnquist describes victim impact evidence as being "designed to portray for the sentencing authority the actual harm caused by a particular crime." However, the Court never explains exactly what role this evidence is to play in the sentencing determination, nor why a "glimpse" of the life extinguished by the defendant's act is a relevant consideration in setting the level of punishment. Even if the Court assumes that the decision to impose the death penalty rather than a lesser punishment may turn on a desire for revenge, it is unclear exactly how evidence of a victim's positive attributes or the impact of the crime on the victim's family is to contribute to the jurors' understanding of the harm caused by the defendant.

The only clear role for this evidence is to serve as a direct appeal to the emotional sympathies of the jurors, or to lead them to base their decision on an assessment of the value of the victim's life and the extent to which a victim is missed by survivors. The *Payne* Court itself acknowledges that both of these roles are unacceptable. The admission of victim impact evidence, particularly if it involves testimony by bereaved family members, greatly increases the risk that the sentencing decision will be made based on passion, whim or prejudice rather than on reasoned deliberation. These are not acceptable bases for decisions anywhere in the criminal justice system, but especially not in capital sentencing trials, in which it is constitutionally required that jury discretion be sufficiently guided to ensure that its decision is not based on such factors. . . .

The concept of grading punishment based on an assessment of the social worth of the victim injects arbitrariness into the sentencing process by allowing various prejudices to influence the sentencing decision. This is not only morally offensive, it also violates the guarantees of equal protection under the law that our system of criminal justice purports to uphold.

Perhaps the most worrisome aspect of the introduction of victim impact evidence is the possibility that it will allow capital sentencing decisions to turn on invidious and constitutionally impermissible factors such as the race or social class of the victim. It has been established statistically that death sentences are given more often to defendants whose victims were white than to defendants whose victims were black. The Court has acknowledged in prior opinions the risk that sentencing can be influenced by racial prejudice.

Misplaced Emphasis

Examining the issue of victim impact evidence that focuses on the grief of family members further clarifies the irrelevance of this evidence to anything but an arbitrarily imposed decision. The idea that it is a greater crime to kill someone who is survived by family members who are greatly bereaved by the loss, and whose family members are willing and able to take the stand and express the impact of the crime in a compelling way, is not explicitly sanctioned by the Court. Moreover, "[s]uch characteristics as the articulateness of family members will often be products of class or wealth, thereby serving as surrogates for impermissible status considerations that no one would claim should influence capital sentencing. . . . By its very nature, [victim impact] evidence invites the jury to 'choose up sides,' to empathize with the (usually more attractive) victim or the victim's family, in particular when these are white, middle-class and otherwise similar to most of the jurors.". . . .

Denying Defendants' Rights

Victims' rights groups have made significant progress by recognizing the plight of victims and increasing sensitivity to victims throughout the criminal process. However, they have also introduced a measure of injustice into the system. While the victim impact statement encourages participation by victims at sentencing, it can prejudice defendants and infringe on their constitutional rights.

Dina R. Hellerstein, *American Criminal Law Review*, vol. 27, no. 2, 1989.

The idea that there should be some sort of "balance" between the defendant's interests and individual victim's interests in a criminal sentencing proceeding contravenes the basic purpose of the proceeding itself. The majority in *Payne* ignores the fact that the purpose of a criminal sentencing proceeding is to make a decision about the *defendant*, not the victim. In response to the majority's argument that it is necessary to allow the state to counter the defendant's mitigating evidence with positive evidence about the victim, Justice John Paul Stevens aptly points out, "[t]his argument is a classic *non sequitur*; the victim is not on trial; her character, whether good or bad, cannot therefore constitute an aggravating or mitigating circumstance." Moreover, if the true aim is to achieve a balance, allowing evidence of the impact of the victim's death on his or her family would mandate that the defendant's family be allowed to testify as to the impact the execution of the defendant would have on them—evidence that the Court would most likely deem completely irrelevant. Most importantly, as Justice Stevens also notes, the scales are not supposed to be weighted evenly between the defendant and the state in criminal trials; the defendant has always been guaranteed certain protections against the disproportionately powerful state.

Payne v. Tennessee represents a significant curtailment of capital defendants' rights under the Eighth Amendment. This decision, with its broad conception of harm caused by a criminal act that need not be related to the defendant's knowledge or intent in committing the act, nor limited to the direct consequences of his or her crime, creates a definition of "relevancy" for evidence that is boundless. As a result of the *Payne* decision and the Court's overruling of *Booth* and *Gathers*, prosecutors can introduce evidence that may have nothing to do with the defendant or the circumstances of the crime committed, but is highly prejudicial and irrefutable by the defendant. The practical result of this decision is that it will become easier for states to sentence criminal defendants to death. Though the *Payne* decision specifically states that unduly inflammatory victim impact evidence can still be challenged under the Due Process Clause of the Fourteenth Amendment, in light of the gradual erosion of capital defendants' rights to appeal their convictions, this thought is not entirely comforting. . . .

The use of victim impact evidence in capital sentencing proceedings, to the extent that it truly vindicates the interests of crime victims or their families, advances victims' interests only at a serious cost to capital defendants' Eighth Amendment rights. While there may indeed be a valid basis for the complaints of victims' rights advocates that our criminal justice system does not adequately serve the needs and interests of crime victims, the true challenge is to devise a way to change the system so that victims' interests can be better served without unduly infringing on defendants' rights. The Court's departure in *Payne* from its earlier holdings that victim impact evidence is per se inadmissible under the Eighth Amendment is not a step in the right direction toward meeting this challenge.

"There is no legitimate constitutional argument, based on the Eighth Amendment, for a per se bar on victim impact evidence. "

Victims' Rights Do Not Threaten Defendants' Rights

Keith L. Belknap Jr.

In the following article, Keith L. Belknap Jr. argues that a defendant's constitutional rights are not violated when the courts use victim impact statements. Belknap contends that such statements are not unfair to the defendant and legitimately uphold the state's interest in providing victims with a way to participate in the criminal justice process. Belknap is an attorney with a Chicago law firm.

As you read, consider the following questions:

1. What did the Supreme Court decide in *Booth v. Maryland* and *South Carolina v. Gathers*, according to Belknap?
2. What are two faulty premises in *Booth* and *Gathers*, according to the author?
3. At what point would the Supreme Court take away a state's privilege to use victim impact evidence, according to Belknap?

From Keith L. Belknap Jr., "The Death Penalty and Victim Impact Evidence: *Payne v. Tennessee*." Reprinted with permission of the *Harvard Journal of Law and Public Policy* 15 (Winter 1992): 275-84.

Over the last few years, the victims' rights movement has persuaded the criminal justice system to heighten its concern for crime victims, particularly during criminal sentencing. The movement's most dramatic achievement to date occurred in *Payne v. Tennessee* [1991], when a newly configured Supreme Court overruled recent precedents and held that the Eighth Amendment erects no *per se* bar to the admission of victim impact evidence in capital sentencing proceedings.

States' Decisions

In two previous decisions, *Booth v. Maryland* [1987] and *South Carolina v. Gathers* [1989], the Supreme Court had dealt serious blows to advocates of victims' rights. In *Booth*, the Court had held five-to-four that admission of victim impact evidence in the sentencing phase of a capital trial violates the Eighth Amendment's prohibition against cruel and unusual punishment. In *Gathers*, the Court extended the rule of *Booth* to a prosecutor's references, when arguing for the death penalty, to the victim's personal characteristics.

In contrast to these decisions, the *Payne* Court correctly reasoned that the States are free to decide that the harm imposed on a victim's family is relevant to the moral blameworthiness of a defendant. The dissenters argued that because victim impact evidence encourages reliance on factors other than the defendant's culpability, such evidence always prejudices the defendant. Although some aspects of the dissenters' arguments may be quite compelling in particular cases, victim impact evidence is not inherently prejudicial, and therefore the admission of such evidence in capital sentencing proceedings does not violate the Eighth Amendment.

Payne involved an especially brutal double homicide. On June 27, 1987, Pervis Tyrone Payne entered the apartment in which Charisse Christopher, her 2-year-old daughter Lacie, and her 3-year-old son Nicholas lived. Payne began making sexual advances toward Charisse. Charisse resisted, and Payne became violent. Payne repeatedly stabbed Charisse and her two children with a butcher knife. Only Nicholas survived the attack. A jury found Payne guilty of two counts of first degree murder and one count of assault with intent to commit murder in the first degree. During the sentencing phase of the trial, Charisse's mother testified that Nicholas regularly cried for his mother and sister. In arguing for the death penalty, the prosecutor commented on the continuing effects of Nicholas' experience. The jury sentenced Payne to death on each of the murder counts and to 30 years in prison for the assault.

On appeal, the Supreme Court of Tennessee affirmed the convictions and sentences. The court found that the grandmother's testimony, although "technically irrelevant" under *Booth*, did not create a risk of arbitrary imposition of the death penalty. The court further held that the prosecutor's closing argument was relevant to Payne's "personal responsibility and moral guilt." The court concluded that any violation of Payne's rights under *Booth* and *Gathers* was harmless error.

TILT

© Liederman/Rothco. Reprinted with permission.

The Supreme Court affirmed the Tennessee Supreme Court's decision. Writing for a six-justice majority, Chief Justice William H. Rehnquist held that "if the State chooses to permit the admission of victim impact evidence and prosecutorial argument on that subject [at the penalty phase of a capital trial], the Eighth Amendment erects no *per se* bar." The majority further held that the Court's decisions to the contrary in *Booth* and *Gathers* were incorrectly decided and explicitly overruled them.

Determining Blameworthiness

The Court first examined the reasoning of *Booth*. In *Booth* the Court noted that although the Court "normally will defer to a state legislature's determination of what factors are relevant to a sentencing decision, the Constitution places some limits on this discretion." The Court emphasized that the Constitution requires a capital defendant to be treated "as a 'uniquely individual human bein[g].'" Accordingly, a determination of sentence must be based on the defendant's "personal responsibility and moral guilt." The Court concluded that because victim impact evidence presents "factors about which the defendant was unaware, and that were irrelevant to the decision to kill," it has no bearing on the "blameworthiness of a particular defendant." The Court also held that victim impact evidence "creates an impermissible risk that the capital sentencing decision will be made in an arbitrary manner."

The *Payne* Court concluded that *Booth* and *Gathers* were based on two faulty premises: (1) the harm caused by the defendant is not relevant to the defendant's blameworthiness; and (2) only evidence relating to blameworthiness is relevant to a capital sentencing decision. The Court pointed out that the harm caused by a defendant historically has been relevant in determining both the particular offense and the appropriate punishment. While acknowledging constitutional limits on a state's discretion in imposing the death penalty, the Court found that "[b]eyond these limitations . . . the Court has deferred to the State's choice of substantive factors relevant to the penalty determination." The Court characterized victim impact evidence as "simply another form or method of informing the sentencing authority about the specific harm caused by the crime in question, evidence of a general type long considered by sentencing authorities.". . .

Having found that a state may properly conclude that the harm caused by an offender's homicide goes to the offender's blameworthiness, the Court further held that such evidence does not necessarily lead to arbitrary impositions of the death penalty. The Court reasoned that if the introduction of victim impact evidence renders a proceeding fundamentally unfair then the Due Process Clause of the Fourteenth Amendment provides a mechanism for relief.

Incorrect Decisions

The Court characterized the doctrine of stare decisis (policy of courts to uphold previously decided cases) as "the preferred course," but found that "when governing decisions are unworkable or are badly reasoned, 'this Court has never felt constrained to follow precedent.'" The Court added that considerations in favor of stare decisis are least significant in cases involving procedural and evidentiary rules. The Court reasoned that *Booth* and *Gathers* "were decided by the narrowest of margins, over spirited dissents challenging the basic underpinnings of those decisions." Based on these circumstances, and the Court's conclusion that these decisions were wrongly decided, the Court explicitly overruled *Booth* and *Gathers*.

The proposition of *Booth* and *Gathers* that victim impact evidence is irrelevant to a capital sentencing decision disregards the Court's own Eighth Amendment jurisprudence and the role that accountability plays in the criminal justice system. The

Court has traditionally applied a proportionality test to cases, arising under the Punishments Clause involving capital punishment. In *Coker v. Georgia* [1977], the Court indicated that

> proportionality—at least as regards capital punishment—not only requires an inquiry into contemporary standards as expressed by legislators and jurors, but also involves the notion that the magnitude of the punishment imposed must be related to the degree of the harm inflicted on the victim. . . .

In rejecting the use of victim impact evidence, the decision in *Booth* ignored the Court's own concern with the harm inflicted on the victim in determining the magnitude of the punishment.

In addition, *Booth* failed to take into account contemporary standards of legislators and jurors. In *Booth*, Justice Powell, writing for the majority, correctly reasoned that the function of a capital sentencing jury is to "express the conscience of the community on the ultimate question of death." If statutes are indeed "first among the objective indicia" of community attitudes, then the moral judgment of most people in this country is that "the amount of harm one causes does bear upon the extent of his 'personal responsibility.'" At the time *Booth* was handed down, "[a]t least thirty-one jurisdictions provide[d] for the use of victim impact evidence in one form or another during the sentencing phase." As of April 1991, "forty-seven states legislatively authorize[d] input by the victim at sentencing." Given the States' widespread use of victim impact evidence, one suspects that the *Booth* majority consulted its own moral judgment rather than that of the community, especially where there was no reason to believe that the jury in *Booth* failed to express the conscience of the community.

No Prejudice to the Defendant

The *Booth* Court's view of relevancy in a capital case is inconsistent with the role of accountability in non-capital cases. The notion that the degree of harm caused by a defendant should influence the severity of punishment pervades the criminal justice system. As Justice Antonin Scalia pointed out, a driver who speeds at sixty miles per hour on a residential street may lose his license if he causes no injury, but may be convicted of manslaughter if a pedestrian happens to be in his path—although his "moral guilt," as defined by *Booth*, would be no greater. The *Booth* Court offered no distinction between capital and non-capital cases that would justify the relevance of victim impact evidence in one context and not in the other. Indeed, there is no precedent, save *Booth*, that argues that victim impact evidence is irrelevant to sentencing considerations.

In contrast to their position on relevancy, the dissenters' arguments based on prejudicial impact initially are quite compelling.

The dissents in *Payne* argued that because victim impact evidence "encourages reliance on emotion and other arbitrary factors," such evidence "necessarily prejudices the defendant." The dissents echoed the *Booth* majority's fears of sentences being imposed as a result of a "'mini-trial' on the victim's character," or "the eloquence with which family members express their grief [or] the status of the victim in the community." The majority did not respond fully to the dissents, and the arguments the majority did offer were not wholly persuasive.

In the absence of a systematic prejudicial effect, however, there is no legitimate constitutional argument, based on the Eighth Amendment, for a *per se* bar on victim impact evidence. As a matter of constitutional law, "the Court has never held 'that the excessively inflammatory character of concededly relevant evidence can form the basis for a constitutional attack. . . .'" Because victim impact evidence is not inherently prejudicial, the balancing of relevance and prejudice is a "state evidentiary issue, which [the Court does] not sit to review." A constitutional issue only arises where evidence is so unduly prejudicial in a particular case that it renders the trial fundamentally unfair under the Due Process Clause of the Fourteenth Amendment.

The System Should Support the Victim

The criminal justice system can stand up for the rights of the innocent victim, rather than blindly and unilaterally protecting the rights of the innocent-until-proven-guilty criminal. The criminal justice system must become a haven for those victimized by those who violate the law, rather than just for those who seek the constitutional protections afforded them in spite of their criminal activity. Those who have dubbed the process the "criminal injustice system" must have new cause to believe in its righteous pursuit of justice fully respective of the needs of innocent victims.

John Heinz, *USA Today Magazine*, July 1984.

The *Payne* dissents also emphasized, and strenuously objected to, the majority's creation of a "radical new exception to the doctrine of *stare decisis*." Justice Thurgood Marshall argued that the "'stron[g] presumption of validity' to which 'recently decided cases' are entitled 'is an essential thread in the mantle of protection that the law affords the individual. . . .'" Justice Scalia responded by quoting the writings of Justice Marshall himself: "[H]owever admirable its resolute adherence to the law as it was, a decision contrary to the public sense of justice as it is, operates, so far as it is known, to diminish respect for the courts and for the law itself." Given that there is no constitutional basis for a broad prophylactic rule excluding all victim impact evidence from capital sentencing proceedings, the *Payne* Court justifiably deferred to the overwhelming public consensus on the relevance of such evidence to capital sentencing.

Extending Victim Impact Evidence

The Court's holdings in *Booth* and *Gathers* were not dictated by precedent, logic, or history; they were the result of a policy choice. In *Payne*, the Court recognized that the determination of who has the better argument on policy with respect to victim impact evidence rightfully belongs to the state legislatures. The conservative six-justice majority's activist stance in overruling recent precedent represents a renewed deference to state legislatures on capital sentencing issues. As a result, many states will likely extend the use of victim impact evidence, which is already prevalent in non-capital trials, to capital sentencing proceedings.

a critical thinking activity

Recognizing Deceptive Arguments

People who feel strongly about an issue use many techniques to persuade others to agree with them. Some of these techniques appeal to the intellect, some to the emotions. Many of them distract the reader or listener from the real issues.

A few common examples of argumentation tactics are listed below. Most of them can be used either to advance an argument in an honest, reasonable way.or to deceive or distract from the real issues. It is important for a critical reader to recognize these tactics in order to rationally evaluate an author's ideas.

 a. *bandwagon*—the idea that "everybody" does this or believes this

 b. *categorical statements*—stating something in a way that implies there can be no argument or disagreement on the issue

 c. *personal attack*—criticizing an opponent personally instead of rationally debating his or her ideas

 d. *testimonial*—quoting or paraphrasing an authority or celebrity to support one's own viewpoint

The following activity can help you sharpen your skills in recognizing deceptive reasoning. The statements below are derived from the viewpoints in this chapter. *Beside each one, mark the letter of the type of deceptive appeal being used. More than one type of tactic may be applicable. If you believe the statement is not any of the listed appeals, write N.*

1. The Supreme Court has a greater obligation to protect the rights of victims than those of criminals.

2. It is clear to every intelligent person that the Eighth Amendment to the U.S. Constitution, protection against cruel and unusual punishment, does not bar the use of victim impact statements.

3. Victim reforms will destroy the constitutional rights of the accused.

4. The conservative, prejudiced Supreme Court judges are too stupid to recognize the rights of the accused.

5. Every decent lawyer believes the harm a victim suffered because of a defendant should be considered when determining punishment.

6. Victims have absolutely no rights at all.

7. Everyone agrees that victim reforms are false promises made by legislators seeking to please voters worried about crime.

8. The victims' rights movement developed because victims of crime felt they had no rights in the criminal justice system.

9. Thurgood Marshall, a pro-criminal, bleeding-heart liberal, considers the harm a victim suffered irrelevant in a criminal trial.

10. As Justice John Paul Stevens correctly points out, the defendant should have more rights than the state in a criminal trial.

11. Victim impact statements force juries to base their decisions on emotion rather than on objective facts.

12. As Deborah Kelly, chair of the American Bar Association's Victims' Committee, accurately concludes, victims' satisfaction with the criminal justice system depends more on how they were treated than how severely their assailants were punished.

13. Everyone knows that judges let criminals off too easily.

14. Intelligent people agree that victims' rights deny the accused the right to a fair and impartial trial.

15. As the Chief Justice of the U.S. Supreme Court, William H. Rehnquist, states, there is no constitutional rule that excludes victim impact statements.

Periodical Bibliography

The following articles have been selected to supplement the diverse views presented in this chapter.

Richard B. Abell — "Victims: An Integral Part of the Criminal Justice System," *Prosecutor*, Spring 1989. Available from the National District Attorneys Association, 1033 N. Fairfax St., Suite 200, Alexandria, VA 22314.

Jill Abramson — "Firm Supports Victims' Role in Death Cases," *The Wall Street Journal*, December 12, 1988.

George M. Anderson — "The Victim's Rights Movement," *California Prisoner*, September 1987. Available from the Prisoners Rights Union, 1909 6th St., Sacramento, CA 95814.

Karen Bokram — "A Special Kind of Help," *Psychology Today*, January/February 1992.

Ted Gest et al. — "Victims of Crime," *U.S. News & World Report*, July 31, 1989.

Andrea Gross — "The Greatest Loss of All," *Ladies Home Journal*, May 1992.

Jeanie Kasindorf — "Victims: The Stories of Seven New Yorkers Caught in the War Zone," *Time*, January 22, 1992.

Debra Kent — "Violated!" *Redbook*, July 1991.

Judith M. Mardorf — "When a Drunk Driver Kills," *Newsweek*, June 10, 1991.

Jeffrie G. Murphy — "Do Crime Victims Have a Right to Get Even?" *The World & I*, April 1991.

Walter Shapiro — "What Say Should Victims Have?" *Time*, May 27, 1991.

Adam Starchild — "Make Victims the Focus of the Law," *Friends Journal*, July 1991. Available from Friends Publishing Corporation, 1501 Cherry St., Philadelphia, PA 19102-1497.

Junda Woo — "Victims' Rights Guide Is Drawn by Legal Group," *The Wall Street Journal*, July 7, 1992.

Joel J. Ziegler — "Must We Victimize Crime Victims?" *The New York Times*, February 27, 1988.

4

How Do Lawyers Affect the Criminal Justice System?

Chapter Preface

In Shakespeare's play *Henry VI*, Part II, Dick, the follower of rebel leader Jack Cade, states: "The first thing we do, let's kill all the lawyers." This famous line is often quoted by those who dislike lawyers and want to vent their frustration with the legal profession. Ironically, taken in context, the line refers to the crucial role of lawyers in society: Dick actually says that the best way to create anarchy is to do away with lawyers.

The two interpretations of this line reflect society's conflicting attitudes about lawyers. While lawyers settle disputes, they also depend on disputes to make their living. Some would say that lawyers' very existence fosters dissension in society. Former attorney Sam Benson supported this view in a November 1991 issue of *Newsweek* when he stated that lawyers spend their time "justifying, exacerbating and inflaming problems." Instead of solving controversies, lawyers have created them to enrich their profession and themselves.

It is also perceived, however, that lawyers merely wage battles that society will not fight on its own. In defending the role of lawyers in society, author Peter Hay states, "Lawyers are surrogate warriors fighting our battles, and they provide convenient if not always fair targets when they lose for us." Hay and others view lawyers as the settlers of disputes that nonlawyers precipitate.

Lawyers, perceived as both the solution to and the cause of conflict, are both admired and despised by society. The authors in this chapter debate the diverse opinions held about the role of lawyers in the criminal justice system.

"It is the lawyer's job to do every possible thing that can be done for the defendant, even when that means getting a criminal off scot-free."

A Case for Defending the Guilty

Lisa J. McIntyre

The American criminal justice system entitles everyone to a defense when they have been accused of a crime. For criminal defense attorneys, it is not a question of whether the criminal defendant is guilty or innocent but whether the system is respecting the rights of all defendants, according to Lisa J. McIntyre. In the following viewpoint, she states that the role of the defense attorney is to force prosecutors to prove guilt beyond a reasonable doubt, give reasonable evidence, and overcome the presumption of innocence for a defendant to be judged guilty. McIntyre contends that defense attorneys guard the defendant's right to be treated fairly. McIntyre is an assistant professor of sociology at Washington State University in Pullman.

As you read, consider the following questions:

1. What do defense attorneys believe prosecutors and judges do to win cases, according to McIntyre?
2. How do defense attorneys keep the system honest, according to the author?
3. Why do defense attorneys believe that the injustices suffered by the accused are worse than what happens to most victims, according to McIntyre?

Hardly anyone will take issue with the idea that everyone, guilty or innocent, is entitled to a fair trial. But beyond this, the views of lawyers and nonlawyers diverge. To the nonlawyer, a fair trial is one that results in convicting the defendant who is factually guilty and acquitting the defendant who is not. But it is the lawyer's job to do every possible thing that can be done for the defendant, even when that means getting a criminal off scot-free. Loopholes and technicalities are defense attorneys' major weapons. Lay people are inclined to feel that using legal tricks to gain acquittals for the guilty is at least morally objectionable, if not reprehensible. What many people want to know is how defense attorneys can live with themselves after they help a guilty person escape punishment. . . .

> Why do I do it? I do it because the day that I start laying down and not doing my job is the day that people who aren't guilty are going to be found guilty, and that person might be you because the whole system will have degenerated to the point where they can arrest and convict you on very little evidence. So I am protecting you, I am protecting the middle-class. (Quote by a defense attorney.)

On the surface, what a defense lawyer does is simply protect the client's rights. But many lawyers transform the nature of the battle. They are not fighting for the freedom of their client per se but to keep the system honest: "It doesn't mean that I want to get everybody off. It means that I try to make sure the state's attorneys meet up to their obligations, which means that the only way they can prove someone guilty is beyond reasonable doubt, with competent evidence, and overcoming the presumption of innocence. If they can do that, then they get a guilty. If they can't do that, then my client deserves to go home."

Defending the Right to Defend

The lawyers' way of "bracketing" their role, of focusing not on the guilt or innocence of their client but on the culpability of the state, transforms circumstances of low or questionable morality into something for which they can legitimately fight. They do not defend simply because their clients have rights but because they believe that those rights have been, are, or will be ignored by others in the criminal justice system. That their adversaries often cheat is taken for granted by public defenders. As one put it, "I expected a fairly corrupt system, and I found one. Here I am representing people who cheat, lie, and steal, and I find the same intellect represented in the police who arrest them, in some of the prosecutors and some of the judges as well.". . .

The sort of cheating to which public defenders attribute their hostility toward police, prosecutors, and judges is something that public defenders say they see a lot. And though such cheat-

ing may be expected, public defenders find it unacceptable—
and are not afraid to say so. It is ironic, but listening to public
defenders talk about their cases and why they do what they do
is like listening to someone who has just been mugged. Public
defenders do feel as if they are often mugged—by the legal system. There is a lot of real and passionate anger: "Some people
said I'd become cynical after a while. Well, I might be more
cynical about some things, but I don't think I have really
changed my attitude. If anything, I might have become a little
more gung ho. You see that there really is an awful lot of injustice. It becomes very real and it's scary. I find myself becoming
very angry in this job, all the time."

Exploring Human Nature

Strange as it may seem, I grew to like to defend men and women
charged with crime. It soon came to be something more than
winning or losing a case. I sought to learn why one man goes one
way and another takes an entirely different road. I became vitally
interested in the causes of human conduct. This meant more
than the quibbling with lawyers and juries, to get or keep money
for a client so that I could take part of what I won or saved for
him: I was dealing with life, with its hopes and fears, its aspira-
tions and despairs. With me it was going to the foundation of mo-
tive and conduct and adjustments for human beings, instead of
blindly talking of hatred and vengeance, and that subtle, indefin-
able quality that men call "justice" and of which nothing really is
known.

Clarence Darrow, 1932.

There is good evidence that the things that public defenders
cite when they complain about police, prosecutorial, and judicial
misconduct do happen but it would be difficult, of course, to determine just how widespread such behaviors actually are. Yet,
the real frequency of misconduct is beside the point. The point is
that most public defenders believe that such things do happen
"all the time. It's something you really have to watch for."
Whether or not public defenders are correct in their assumptions that police lie, that prosecutors will often do anything to
win, and that judges do not really care or know enough to be fair,
it is quite clear that the way in which the public defenders see
the world not only excuses their work but makes it seem important. Their rationales are enabling mechanisms for the public defenders. But what ultimately pushes the lawyer to do the job is, I
believe, something even more personal—the desire to win. . . .

On television a defense lawyer confronts his clients with demands for the truth: "Okay, I'm your lawyer and you gotta trust me. If I am going to do a good job I need to know exactly what happened. Don't be afraid to tell me, I can't defend you unless you are perfectly straight with me." The client is thus persuaded to tell all to his lawyer.

This sort of dialogue may appeal to the viewer's common sense—that is, of course the lawyer needs to know what happened and whether the client is guilty. But in real life, things do not happen that way—at least they *do not* happen that way when the lawyer is a public defender. Public defenders are quick to admit that they usually do not ask their clients whether they are guilty or innocent. Why not ask? The lawyers claimed that it was simply not relevant, that it was something that they did not need to know. . . .

> I do not apologize for (or feel guilty about) helping to let a murderer go free—even though I realize that someday one of my clients may go out and kill again. Since nothing like that has ever happened, I cannot know for sure how I would react. I know that I would feel terrible for the victim. But I hope that I would not regret what I had done—any more than a surgeon should regret saving the life of a patient who recovers and later kills an innocent victim. (Alan Dershowitz, 1983.)

Doctors lose patients; lawyers lose cases. Failure is something with which every professional must cope. But implicit in the question, How can you defend those people?, is the idea that public defenders ought to have trouble coping with winning.

Gaining a New Perspective

The possibility of getting a guilty person off is not a specter that haunts public defenders, at least not to the extent that you would notice it. In misdemeanor and juvenile courts, the majority of defendants represented by public defenders are relatively innocent and/or harmless criminals accused of relatively innocent or harmless crimes. The lawyers are protected by the fact that they rarely win cases for clients who are horrible criminals; winning an acquittal for a burglar or even an armed robber is, for a public defender, hardly cause for intense introspective examinations of one's morality or personal guilt. It is not that they have lost all sense of proportion but that they have gained a new one—by the time that they get to felony courtrooms, the lawyers are, most of them, convinced that what they see happen to their clients in the jails or in the courts is as bad as or worse than most of what happens to victims out on the streets. There is, moreover, often a sense that the injustices perpetrated by the system are worse because they are committed by people who really ought to know better. . . .

[Public defenders] believe that it is right to defend "those

141

people" because of the principle that everyone is innocent until proved otherwise and so everyone is entitled to a defense. More important, they also believe that it is right to defend even the guilty because their clients *need* someone to defend them against police, prosecutorial, and judicial abuse. Because of what they see happen in the system every day, public defenders would be the last to claim that defense lawyers are unnecessary luxuries for defendants (guilty or innocent) in our criminal courts.

> "I finally felt that I could no longer defend criminal cases with a clear conscience."

A Case for Not Defending the Guilty

Marion S. Rosen

In the following viewpoint, Marion S. Rosen argues that the criminal justice system favors criminal defendants and allows violent criminals to be released early from jail. Rosen, a former defense attorney, describes how she questioned her role of defending the guilty and decided she could no longer assist in helping criminals escape justice. Rosen is an attorney working for victims' rights in Houston, Texas.

As you read, consider the following questions:

1. What attitudes of criminals made Rosen want to quit as a defense attorney?
2. Why does the author believe she is not alone in her feelings about being a defense attorney?
3. What does Rosen suggest should be done to deter others from leaving the defense field?

Marion S. Rosen, "A Defense Lawyer's Adieu," *The National Law Journal*, June 1, 1992, pp. 19-21. Copyright © 1992, the New York Law Publishing Co. Reprinted with permission.

When the count reached two murdered, three assaulted, four raped, five victims of robbery—not to count burglaries, auto thefts and other violent and non-violent crimes—amongst friends and acquaintances, I then decided it was time to re-evaluate my professional goals.

Getting Away with Crime

No longer did I want to be part of a system that not only allowed, but was clearly fostering, an attitude that the violent criminal could get away with a crime and that the punishment would be so minor that there was no deterrence from committing the offense. The vast majority of crimes were being committed by recidivists. Not only in Texas, but throughout many states, criminals were a part of early release programs that were allowing them to return to society when they had not even served their court-ordered time as a means of punishment. The system no longer was working.

When I initially started in the practice of criminal law in Texas, those convicted served approximately two-thirds of their sentences. Today in Texas, a convict will serve approximately 26 days for each year of his sentence. Criminals were thumbing their noses at society because of the brief period of time that they were being compelled to serve a sentence. Many of those accused who were in our county jails, who were unable to post bond and had attorneys appointed to represent them, were released at the time they pleaded guilty.

Harris County, Texas, where Houston is centered, became Texas' busiest hub for halfway houses that were being used for pre-parole transfers. State of Texas authorities set up halfway houses in Houston rather than in more rural areas. In Houston alone, there are 306 beds in halfway houses. That represents more than 40 percent of the 761 beds in halfway houses in Harris County. Therefore, very quickly, Harris County became the dumping ground for the worst offenders.

I tired of hearing the prison inmates complaining about having too few television sets, too many TV sets, not enough TV noise or too much TV noise. Letters were sent to governmental authorities, and lawsuits were filed for violation of inmates' civil rights. Suits of this sort helped to tie up court dockets. Meanwhile, nobody was speaking out for the victims.

Revolving-Door Policy

I became negative about my role in extending the criminal justice process. I realized that I could no longer work to help put these people back on the street to continue to commit these violent acts. I am not saying that the accused are not entitled to a defense because certainly everyone is entitled to a defense in ac-

144

cordance with our system, but if one's heart is not in it, one cannot be effective. I started feeling wrong about what I was doing in prolonging a process that was headed down a one-way street.

Apparently, I am not alone in the decision I made. In Texas, the State Bar's Criminal Justice Section has lost 25 percent of its 1,504 members since 1986. The Texas Criminal Defense Lawyers Association gained a mere 100 members, raising their membership from 1,250 to 1,350 in Texas, although 7,340 lawyers initiated the practice of law in Texas in that same period.

Guilty Clients' Lies

A criminal lawyer was surrounded by lies. Clients, witnesses, paid experts (such as psychiatrists), prosecutors—everybody—it seemed, lied or could be lying. Except me . . . most of the time . . . as far as I could tell. . . .

My initial response had been to overlook the fact that defendants lie, or, if I could not overlook it, to forgive them for it somehow. In a perverse way, I didn't feel it was as outrageous for them to lie as for other people. Defendants were desperately trying to stay out of prison, and I could sympathize with that desire after having spent so much time in prisons myself, as a visitor.

Seymour Wishman, *Confessions of a Criminal Lawyer*, 1981.

In 1990, statistics on violent crime reflected an increase in Houston and throughout the United States. And in 1991, there was an estimated surge of 59 percent of rapes and attempted rapes with a substantial increase in assaults, according to a Justice Department survey. Of the 8,000 sex offenders in prison in Texas, only a few hundred receive some treatment.

The revolving-door policy of our prisons does not seem to work because the early release of parolees is placing these offenders on the street with no regard for the safety of the public. This creates a pervasive sense of fear throughout a community. Why isn't the public protected from the violent criminals who prey upon society? When violent offenders dictate our quality of life, we do not live in a civilized society.

A Change in Direction

Fed up with the system that freed inmates too early, I finally felt that I could no longer defend criminal cases with a clear conscience. Having made the decision, I feel that it is well thought out and the right one for me. I find that I breathe more comfortably and sleep more restfully, having made this decision.

Since then, I have turned my attention now to representing

victims of criminal and civil attacks in civil litigation, harassment, discrimination and other tort litigation, as well as the family law that I have been engaged in for about 20 years.

It is unlikely that I will return to criminal defense, but if other lawyers are not to be deterred as I have been, we must address this area of law and find new ways to make punishment work as a tool for reform. At the risk of sounding Pollyanna-ish, I firmly believe that we need to reassess our values and morals, beginning with family relationships. Perhaps, too, we need to participate in closer supervision and counseling of our young people and their peers.

And, on a practical note, perhaps we need mandatory sentencing, with penalties that are to be served to the fullest possible extent. In Louisiana, where convicted felons serve out sentences and there are no early release programs, statistics confirm that violent crime has been reduced. Certainly, it is far less frequent there than it is here, in Texas.

> *"There is a great deal of good that lawyers do for our society."*

Lawyers Strengthen the Legal System

Peter Hay

Lawyers have received undeserved criticism, according to Peter Hay. In the following viewpoint, Hay argues that lawyers are modern day warriors who fight our legal battles in court. In addition, he maintains that lawyers fight to uphold individual rights and promote change within the government. Hay, the editor of *The Book of Legal Anecdotes*, is a free-lance writer residing in Los Angeles, California.

As you read, consider the following questions:

1. How does the author address the contention that society has too many lawyers?
2. Why does the U.S. Constitution favor criminal defendants, according to Hay?
3. What four qualities do lawyers possess that society in general lacks, in Hay's opinion?

Peter Hay, "Why We Love to Hate Lawyers." This article originally appeared in the September 23, 1989, *Los Angeles Times*. The author revised it in October 1992 for inclusion in the present volume.

Lawyer-bashing has been on the increase in the United States, which has by far the largest number of attorneys per capita in the world. They are blamed for a range of ills in a clogged justice system: the law's delays, the high cost of liability insurance and runaway jury awards. They are accused of enriching themselves through the misery of others; of lacking principles because they can take either side of an issue; and of exercising too much influence in every sphere of social and political endeavor. There are far too many lawyers, we are told, as if this was some natural catastrophe, like an unexpected swarm of locusts or killer bees. Bestselling novelist Tom Clancy was quoted in *Newsweek* that "a lawyer is just like an attack dog, only without a conscience." One of the popular jokes of recent years asks why lawyers made better laboratory experiments than rats. Three reasons are given: With lawyers there'd be no shortage of experimental subjects; no danger of getting attached to them, and finally, there are some jobs that you can't get rats to perform.

Fighting Our Battles

Of course, anti-lawyer sentiment is by no means peculiar to our times. Master Peter Pathelin, in the French medieval farce of the same title, is shown as a thief and a cheat, who is treated to a dose of his own medicine. The mob in Shakespeare's *Henry VI, Pt. 2* rallies to the cry "The first thing we do, let's kill all the lawyers," from Dick the Butcher, to which the rebel leader Jack Cade responds: "Is not this a lamentable thing, that the skin of an innocent lamb should be made parchment? that parchment, being scribbled o'er, should undo a man?" And Hamlet, communing with the dust of poor Yorick, asks: "Why may not that be the skull of a lawyer? Where be his quiddities now, his quillets, his cases, his tenures, and his tricks?" Even the popular joke about the lawyer thrown overboard, who is left unharmed by the sharks because of professional courtesy, goes back in one version to eighteenth-century London.

Yet, there is a troubling aspect to the current outbreak of sick jokes, quite apart from their general lack of good humor. Sticks and stones often follow name-calling, and we should be reminded of recent history, when certain groups were first designated as vermin in order to justify their extermination later.

Not that lawyers are an endangered species, or need a layman like myself to defend them. But the supply of lawyers is ample, I would argue, because of an ever-increasing demand for them. Neither their number nor their ubiquity are accidents of nature. We have invited lawyers to attend every significant phase of our private life, from acquiring surrogate babies, arranging marriage contracts and divorce settlements, to transferring property, redressing real injury or perceived discrimination, to cope with the consequences of death and taxes. We use lawyers to live and do business with each other, and also to avoid one another. Because we are basically cowardly, who seek but hate confrontation, lawyers become surrogate warriors fighting our battles, and they provide convenient, if not always fair targets for impotent rage when they lose for us, as statistically they must in fifty percent of all cases. When our lawyer wins, he or she remains in our good graces, partly because the losing side pays all the costs. When we lose, however, we resent paying even our own side's fees and contingencies to which we had agreed so readily when we were bursting to get at the other fellow.

Protecting Our Rights

Contrary to received opinion, a good lawyer is more likely to try and dissuade an over-heated client from litigation, or offer to arbitrate and settle, than to perform the role of an attack dog. "Discourage litigation," Abraham Lincoln once advised his colleagues: "Persuade your neighbors to compromise whenever you can. Point out to them how the nominal winner is often a real loser—in fees, expenses, and waste of time. As a peacemaker, the lawyer has a superior opportunity of becoming a good man. There will always be business."

Valuable Contribution to Society

Lawyers contribute significantly to personal freedom and democracy—social goods that are missed in measures of economic performance. And in a complex, highly mobile society like ours, lawyers add value by devising ways for economic actors to achieve lower transaction costs in a context of imperfect information. Undoubtedly there are ways to provide legal services more efficiently and distribute them more fairly, but we can rest assured that America's high lawyer population has not undermined its economy.

Charles R. Epp, *The Wall Street Journal*, July 9, 1992.

Like Lincoln, two-thirds of the men we have elected president have been lawyers, and for the first time in American history we now have a First Couple, the firm of Hillary and Bill Clinton, representing our interests from the White House. Lincoln also practiced what he preached. Once he warned two farmers who came to see him about a boundary dispute that going to court "will cost both of your farms, and will entail an enmity that will last for generations and perhaps lead to murder." Then he locked them into a room, while he went off to lunch.

149

"Finding ourselves shut up together, we began to laugh," one of the farmers recounted. "That put us in good humor, and by the time Mr. Lincoln returned, the matter was settled."

We have so many lawyers because so many of us need to be locked up, and not just for an hour or two, before we might listen to reason. While so much of the resentment we store up against attorneys in supporting or opposing us arises from petty squabbles, we forget the countless good fights lawyers have helped us all win in the march towards greater equity and justice: by the drafting and passing of good legislation, the successful prosecution of criminals, by winning acquittal for the unjustly accused. We overlook the jurists jailed for their principles or the judges who lose their lives in Colombia and Sicily because of our drug habits.

We may feel frustrated when the criminal justice system seems to protect the rights of criminals more than those of victims, and yet few of us would want to live under a system where a person is assumed to be guilty unless proven innocent, or where the accused is not provided with legal counsel, as the Sixth Amendment in the Bill of Rights insists. You may blame lawyers for holding up sometimes for years the execution of a convicted criminal, but we have to imagine ourselves as that individual on death row, and that possibly we might have got there by mistake.

Lawyers possess that kind of imagination, and the best of them can make members of the jury exercise theirs, thereby raising reasonable doubts in their mind. Of course, it would be much more efficient to operate the justice system only with government witnesses or police testimony, with the guilt and fate of the accused as a foregone conclusion. Fortunately, the framers and interpreters of the U.S. Constitution thought otherwise, and they deliberately tilted the system in favor of the individual rather than towards the state. Many of the techniques that lawyers use to protect a particular individual's rights do seem like a waste of time and money. But even the mediocre and the lazy among them fulfill an independent and essential role in safeguarding our collective freedom.

A Noble Profession

Even when life or liberty are not directly at stake, there is a great deal of good that lawyers do for our society that goes unappreciated. I wonder if attorneys are hated precisely for the opposite reasons that the anti-lawyer jokes imply. Not for their alleged greed or survival instincts, but because of their superb adaptability and mental agility. After all, persuasion by logic and rhetoric, coolness under fire, playing by the rules, respect for precedent—all these qualities that were once applauded as the crowning accomplishments of a cultivated mind—are now confined to shabby unattended courtrooms, where lawyers display their virtuosity to uncomprehending Philistines.

"Law sharpens a man's mind by narrowing it," wrote Edmund Burke in the eighteenth century, but in our world, where only specialists can talk to each other, lawyers have survived and thrived as adaptive generalists. Among my acquaintance lawyers pursue, on the whole, a wider range of hobbies, display broader concerns about public issues, and lead fuller, busier lives than most of the artists, writers, or academics I know. Although they tend to be conservative by training or habits of mind, it is lawyers who often instigate, support, and codify the yearning for social change. Our public institutions, non-profit organizations, modern government itself—all are inconceivable without lawyers, many of whom work at a lower salary than they could earn in the private sector. (Strange to say, but I cannot think of nurses, teachers, or others in the helping professions who do as much work *pro bono* as lawyers perform.)

By holding lawyers and legislators in low esteem, we undermine ourselves and our political system, which needs a steady supply of idealistic, bright people to fight for progressive change. But after entrusting, somewhat cynically, our public affairs to leaders who were openly hostile to the aims of government, we may be turning back for help to those who are passionately interested in making government work. Many of these public-spirited people are lawyers, and we should feel grateful for them. As Adlai Stevenson once quipped to President Kennedy, who kept raiding his office to staff Camelot: "I regret that I have but one law firm to give to my country."

The defense rests.

"Too many lawyers are more committed to their own economic interests than to a sensible legal system."

Lawyers Hamper the Legal System

Robert J. Samuelson

While lawyers are supposed to prevent and resolve conflicts, most incite conflicts in order to make money, according to Robert J. Samuelson. In the following viewpoint, Samuelson argues that lawyers have lost the true purpose of their profession. Motivated only by profit, lawyers have created an illusion that all disputes can be handled legally. Consequently, society has an overabundance of lawyers who do not care about justice and have clogged the courts with frivolous lawsuits, according to the author. Samuelson is a contributing editor for *Newsweek* magazine.

As you read, consider the following questions:

1. What change does Samuelson say the U.S. legal system should adopt? Why is it better?
2. Why do most American lawyers hate the English rule, according to the author?
3. What might force lawyers to change the system, according to Samuelson?

I wrote my first and last law-review article in 1986. You can look it up: *Maryland Law Review*, Vol. 46, No. 1, pages 78-85. Actually, it's only a brief comment on a windy treatise by a genuine law professor. As far as I can tell, no one ever read my short reply. Still, it plugged a good idea: the "English rule."

Motivated by Conflict

I am a lawyer-basher and proud of it. Most American lawyers abhor the English rule. It requires the losing side in a civil suit to pay the winning side's attorneys' costs. This approach would discourage weak or frivolous suits, while encouraging defendants to settle strong suits against them. More generally, it would promote new and less costly ways of resolving conflicts aside from litigation.

What's wrong with lawyers is that they have an economic interest in cultivating and prolonging conflict. This means they are fundamentally at odds with the purposes of the legal system. Courts and lawyers exist only to explain and enforce the rules society sets for itself—and settle disputes arising from these rules. Ideally, the system should minimize conflicts by ensuring that the rules are clear and that disagreements are resolved rapidly. The trouble is that lawyers' well-being runs in the opposite direction. The more conflict, the better. The more cumbersome and ambiguous society's rules, the better.

The increase in crime, divorce, regulations and government accounts for much of the rise in lawyering. But things have gone beyond that. Lawyers pander to the American illusion that all problems have legal solutions, and the result is a society that requires lawyers to do almost anything. We now have more than twice as many of them as in 1970 (805,000 in 1990 versus 355,000 in 1970). Our courts are clogged. In 1990, the number of cases filed in state courts topped 100 million.

A lot of the congestion reflects soaring criminal cases; in the federal courts, criminal filings have increased 69 percent since 1980. It's not helpful, though, to whine (as the American Bar Association does) that the court system is "starved for resources" or plagued by "underfunding." The proper response is to ask: can we unclog the system—use it more wisely—by slowing the stream of other disputes that reach court? The answer is "yes."

Our civil-justice system begs for improvement. What we are talking about here is a wide array of suits for private damages. Contracts. Personal injury. Product liability. Medical malpractice. Employment discrimination (racial, sexual and age). Fraud. Libel. Environmental damage. The list of activities subject to litigation has mushroomed. As society's sensibilities have broadened, new laws have established more "rights." In addition, lawyers have effectively created other rights by persuading courts to expand legal doctrines: for example, "wrongful termination" (in effect, being fired unreasonably).

An Abused System

Up to a point, these new rights represent a major advance. They empower individuals and protect us against huge, potentially arbitrary bureaucracies. The threat of being sued can be a useful social discipline. But the recourse to law must also operate smoothly and sensibly. Otherwise, new rights may be more theoretical than real. Or their existence may impose other large costs on society. The civil-justice system now invites just such abuses.

"Of course there are a lot of lawyers. There are just as many criminals."

It encourages suits and legal delays. Consider a simple example. A sues B for $100. Assume that A's case is weak, but that defending it will cost B $20. There's a powerful incentive for B to settle for $19.99. Next, assume that A's case is strong—and that B knows it. Now B is tempted to stretch out the case, increasing A's costs to force a smaller settlement (say $50). The English rule minimizes these problems. In my first example, B might not settle A's weak case. If A pursues the case and loses, A pays B's attorneys' fees. Chances are that A wouldn't bring the case. (In my scheme, a contingency-fee lawyer—who shares any award or settlement—would pay the other side's attorneys' fees in a losing case.) In the second example, B might not delay. If A wins, B would pay both a higher award and A's attorneys' fees.

Naturally, lawyers detest the English rule. It would force them and their clients to evaluate the merits of a case, rather than "gaming" the system. It would prod them to cut litigation costs (less discovery, fewer depositions) and to resort to "alternative dispute resolution" (mediation, arbitration or mock trials). The usual objection to the English rule—that it would prevent suits by poor people against big companies—is a straw horse. No poor person can actually sue a big company today. Suits are effectively brought and financed by contingency-fee lawyers. They could still easily bring strong suits. But bringing weak suits would be riskier and potentially more expensive.

High Costs

Much of the legal system now exists for the well-being of lawyers and only incidentally for clients. The social costs transcend actual litigation. The protracted nature of legal disputes exacts an enormous psychological toll on people, regardless of who wins. The rising threat of suits feeds mistrust and inspires more elaborate contracts. There's more precautionary behavior: defensive medicine is practiced; new products are withheld, if they might somehow provoke a suit. All this requires more lawyers. The biggest—and least visible—cost may be all the talent that is drained into an essentially unproductive occupation.

Lawyer-bashing is increasingly popular. More companies are trying to cut legal bills. [Former] Vice President Quayle condemned lawyers for their costly ways. The Bush administration proposed a small experiment with the English rule. A few lawyers even tout it publicly. "I would think real, real seriously about adopting the English rule," says lawyer and novelist Scott Turow ("Presumed Innocent") in a *Business Week* story on legal reform.

It's doubtful any of this will lead to more than cosmetic reforms. Too many legislators are lawyers. Too many lawyers are more committed to their own economic interests than to a sensible legal system. As a group, lawyers simply won't face the contradiction between their incomes and their professional responsibilities. The only real hope for change comes from a small but rising number of (yes) legal malpractice suits. If enough lawyers become victims of today's system, they may grasp the wisdom of changing it.

"The awesome power that prosecutors exercise is susceptible of abuse."

Prosecuting Attorneys Abuse Their Power

Bennett L. Gershman

Prosecutors can easily abuse their power and are rarely accountable for their actions, according to Bennett L. Gershman, a professor of law at Pace University in White Plains, New York. In the following viewpoint, Gershman argues that prosecutors abuse their power when they threaten to bring additional charges if a defendant refuses to plead guilty, hide evidence to win cases, and initiate charges for personal reasons. He states that it is impossible to prove prosecutorial misconduct because the system protects the prosecutor.

As you read, consider the following questions:

1. Why does Gershman say it is hard to prove that a prosecutor initiated a charge out of personal vindictiveness?
2. What are three harmful effects that result when the prosecution refuses to admit evidence that would set an accused free, according to the author?
3. What are three suggestions Gershman gives in order to punish prosecutors who suppress evidence?

Bennett L. Gershman, "Abuse of Power in the Prosecutor's Office." This article appeared in the June 1991 issue and is reprinted with permission from *The World & I*, a publication of The Washington Times Corporation, © 1991.

The prosecutor is the most dominant figure in the American criminal justice system. As the Supreme Court observed, "Between the private life of the citizen and the public glare of criminal accusation stands the prosecutor. [The prosecutor has] the power to employ the full machinery of the State in scrutinizing any given individual." Thus, the prosecutor decides whether or not to bring criminal charges; whom to charge; what charges to bring; whether a defendant will stand trial, plead guilty, or enter a correctional program in lieu of criminal charges; and whether to confer immunity from prosecution. In jurisdictions that authorize capital punishment, the prosecutor literally decides who shall live and who shall die. Moreover, in carrying out these broad functions, the prosecutor enjoys considerable independence from the courts, administrative superiors, and the public. A prosecutor cannot be forced to bring criminal charges, or be prevented from bringing them. Needless to say, the awesome power that prosecutors exercise is susceptible of abuse. Such abuses most frequently occur in connection with the prosecutor's power to bring charges; to control the information used to convict those on trial; and to influence juries.

Abuse of Power

The prosecutor's charging power includes the virtually unfettered discretion to invoke or deny punishment, and therefore the power to control and destroy people's lives. Such prosecutorial discretion has been called "tyrannical," "lawless," and "most dangerous." Prosecutors may not unfairly select which persons to prosecute. But this rule is difficult to enforce, and the courts almost always defer to the prosecutor's discretion. In one recent case, for example, a prosecutor targeted for prosecution a vocal opponent of the Selective Service system who refused to register, rather than any of nearly a million nonvocal persons who did not register. The proof showed that the defendant clearly was selected for prosecution not because he failed to register but because he exercised his First Amendment rights. This was a legally impermissible basis for prosecution. Nevertheless, the courts refused to disturb the prosecutor's decision, because there was no clear proof of prosecutorial bad faith. Many other disturbing examples exist of improper selection based on race, sex, religion, and the exercise of constitutional rights. These cases invariably are decided in the prosecutor's favor. The reasoning is circular. The courts presume that prosecutors act in good faith, and that the prosecutor's expertise, law enforcement plans, and priorities are ill suited to judicial review.

Unfair selectivity is one of the principal areas of discretionary abuse. Another is prosecutorial retaliation in the form of increased charges after defendants raise statutory or constitutional

157

claims. Prosecutors are not allowed to be vindictive in response to a defendant's exercise of rights. Nevertheless, proving vindictiveness, as with selectiveness, is virtually impossible. Courts simply do not probe the prosecutor's state of mind. For example, prosecutors often respond to a defendant's unwillingness to plead guilty to a crime by bringing higher charges. In one recent case, a defendant charged with a petty offense refused to plead guilty despite prosecutorial threats to bring much higher charges. The prosecutor carried out his threat and brought new charges carrying a sentence of life imprisonment. The court found the prosecutor's conduct allowable. Although the prosecutor behaved in a clearly retaliatory fashion, the court nevertheless believed that the prosecutor needed this leverage to make the system work. If the prosecutor could not threaten defendants by "upping the ante," so the court reasoned, there would be fewer guilty pleas and the system would collapse.

Appealing to Passions

Prosecutors know that appeals to the jury's passions and prejudices, although improper, may skew the jury's evaluation of the proof toward conviction. To that end, prosecutors have displayed inflammatory and inadmissible physical evidence before juries; offered gruesome and irrelevant photographs of the victim; elicited inflammatory testimony; and injected gratuitous, inflammatory rhetoric into the proceedings.

Summation gives the prosecutor a unique opportunity to prejudice the defendant. Common examples of inflammatory argument include exhorting juries to win the war on crime; inciting them to vengeance; using insulting and abusive epithets and invective to describe the defendant; appealing to racial, ethnic, national, or religious prejudice; appealing to wealth and class bias; and imputing to the defendant violence and threats against witnesses.

Bennett L. Gershman, *Trial*, April 1992.

Finally, some prosecutions are instituted for illegitimate personal objectives as opposed to ostensibly valid law enforcement objectives. Such prosecutions can be labeled demagogic and usually reveal actual prosecutorial malice or evil intent. Telltale signs of demagoguery often include the appearance of personal vendettas, political crusades, and witch hunts. Examples of this base practice abound. They have involved prosecutions based on racial or political hostility; prosecutions motivated by personal and political gain; and prosecutions to discourage or coerce the exercise of constitutional rights. One notorious example was New Orleans District Attorney James Garrison's prosecution of Clay Shaw for the Kennedy assassination. Other examples have included the prosecutions of labor leader James Hoffa, New York attorney Roy Cohn, and civil rights leader Dr. Martin Luther King.

Hiding the Evidence

A prosecutor's misuse of power also occurs in connection with legal proof. In the course of an investigation, in pretrial preparation, or even during a trial, prosecutors often become aware of information that might exonerate a defendant. It is not unusual for the prosecutor to have such proof, in view of the acknowledged superiority of law enforcement's investigative resources and its early access to crucial evidence. The adversary system relies on a fair balance of opposing forces. But one of the greatest threats to rational and fair fact-finding in criminal cases comes from the prosecutor's hiding evidence that might prove a defendant's innocence. Examples of prosecutorial suppression of exculpatory evidence are numerous. Such conduct is pernicious for several reasons: It skews the ability of the adversary system to function properly by denying to the defense crucial proof; it undermines the public's respect for and confidence in the public prosecutor's office; and it has resulted in many defendants being unjustly convicted, with the consequent loss of their liberty or even their lives. . . .

To be sure, disclosure is the one area above all else that relies on the prosecutor's good faith and integrity. If the prosecutor hides evidence, it is likely that nobody will ever know. The information will lay buried forever in the prosecutor's files. Moreover, most prosecutors, if they are candid, will concede that their inclination in this area is not to reveal information that might damage his or her case. Ironically, in this important area in which the prosecutor's fairness, integrity, and good faith are so dramatically put to the test, the courts have defaulted. According to the courts, the prosecutor's good or bad faith in secreting evidence is irrelevant. It is the character of the evidence that counts, not the character of the prosecutor. Thus, even if a violation is deliberate, and with an intent to harm the defendant, the courts will not order relief unless the evidence is so crucial that it would have changed the verdict. Thus, there is no real incentive for prosecutors to disclose such evidence.

Hopefully, in light of the disclosures of prosecutorial misconduct, courts, bar associations, and even legislatures will wake up to the quagmire in criminal justice. These bodies should act vigorously and aggressively to deter and punish the kinds of violations that recur all too frequently. Thus, reversals should be required automatically for deliberate suppression of evidence, and the standards for reversal for nondeliberate suppression relaxed; disciplinary action against prosecutors should be the rule rather than the exception; and legislation should be enacted making it a crime for prosecutors to willfully suppress evidence resulting in a defendant's conviction.

Misbehaving in Court

Finally, the prosecutor's trial obligations often are violated. The duties of the prosecuting attorney during a trial were well stated in a classic opinion fifty years ago. The interest of the prosecutor, the court wrote, "is not that it shall win a case, but that justice shall be done. As such, he is in a peculiar and very definite sense the servant of the law, the twofold aim of which is that guilt shall not escape or innocence suffer. He may prosecute with earnestness and vigor—indeed, he should do so. But, while he may strike hard blows, he is not at liberty to strike a foul one."

A Terrifying Problem

Prosecutors are generally perceived by juries as prestigious and honorable "champions of justice." They have powerful strategic and financial resources that usually give them distinct advantages over their adversaries. And prosecutors operate under higher ethical standards than other lawyers—i.e., a special obligation "to seek justice." Despite or because of these differences, prosecutorial misconduct is all too often overlooked, condoned, or found to be harmless.

Prosecutors function in a variety of contexts in the criminal justice system. They enjoy vast decision-making powers in areas such as charging crimes, plea bargaining, granting immunity, summoning witnesses to grand juries, and determining sentences. Prosecutorial domination over the "awful instruments of the criminal law," to use Justice Felix Frankfurter's apt terminology, is largely uncontrolled by the courts. Indeed, unfettered prosecutorial discretion may be the most terrifying and the most insoluble problem in the administration of criminal justice.

Bennett L. Gershman, *Trial*, April 1992.

Despite this admonition, prosecutors continually strike "foul blows." In one leading case of outrageous conduct, a prosecutor concealed from the jury in a murder case the fact that a pair of undershorts with red stains on it, a crucial piece of evidence, was stained not by blood but by paint. In another recent case, a prosecutor, in his summation, characterized the defendant as an "animal," told the jury that "the only guarantee against his future crimes would be to execute him," and that he should have "his face blown away by a shotgun." In another case, the prosecutor argued that the defendant's attorney knew the defendant was guilty; otherwise he would have put the defendant on the witness stand.

The above examples are illustrative of common practices today, and the main reason such misconduct occurs is quite simple: It works. Indeed, several studies have shown the importance of oral advocacy in the courtroom, as well as the effect produced by such conduct. For example, a student of trial advocacy often is told of the importance of the opening statement. Prosecutors would undoubtedly agree that the opening statement is indeed crucial. In a University of Kansas study, the importance of the opening statement was confirmed. From this study, the authors concluded that in the course of any given trial, the jurors were affected most by the first strong presentation that they saw. This finding leads to the conclusion that if a prosecutor were to present a particularly strong opening argument, the jury would favor the prosecution throughout the trial. Alternatively, if the prosecutor were to provide a weak opening statement followed by a strong opening statement by the defense, then, according to the authors, the jury would favor the defense during the trial. It thus becomes evident that the prosecutor will be best served by making the strongest opening argument possible, thereby assisting the jury in gaining a better insight into what they are about to hear and see. The opportunity for the prosecutor to influence the jury at this point in the trial is considerable, and many prosecutors use this opportunity to their advantage, even if the circumstances do not call for lengthy or dramatic opening remarks. . . .

A Fine Line

A final point when analyzing why prosecutorial misconduct persists is the unavailability or inadequacy of penalties visited upon the prosecutor personally in the event of misconduct. Punishment in our legal system comes in varying degrees. An appellate court can punish a prosecutor by simply cautioning him not to act in the same manner again, reversing his case, or, in some cases, identifying by name the prosecutor who misconducted himself. Even these punishments, however, may not be sufficient to dissuade prosecutors from acting improperly. One noteworthy case describes a prosecutor who appeared before the appellate court on a misconduct issue for the third time, each instance in a different case.

Perhaps the ultimate reason for the ineffectiveness of the judicial system in curbing prosecutorial misconduct is that prosecutors are not personally liable for their misconduct. During the course of a trial, the prosecutor is absolutely shielded from any civil liability that might arise due to his or her misconduct, even if that misconduct was performed with malice. To be sure, there is clearly a necessary level of immunity accorded all government officials. Without such immunity, much of what is normally done by officials in authority might not be performed, out of fear that their practices would later be deemed harmful or improper. Granting prosecutors a certain level of immunity is reasonable. Allowing prosecutors to be completely shielded from civil liability in the event of misconduct, however, provides no deterrent to courtroom misconduct.

For the prosecutor, the temptation to cross over the allowable ethical limit must often be tremendous, because of the distinct advantages that such misconduct creates with respect to assisting the prosecutor to win his case by effectively influencing the jury. Most prosecutors must inevitably be subject to this temptation. It takes a constant effort on the part of every prosecutor to maintain the high moral standards necessary to avoid such temptations. Despite the frequent occurrences of courtroom misconduct, appellate courts have not provided significant incentives to deter it. Inroads will not be made in the effort to end prosecutorial misconduct until the courts decide to take a stricter, more consistent approach to this problem.

"[Prosecutors] have diligently and ethically fulfilled their roles."

Prosecuting Attorneys Do Not Abuse Their Power

Brigitte A. Bass

Prosecutors act in the interest of the state to bring charges against individuals suspected of committing a crime. In the following viewpoint, Brigitte A. Bass argues that most prosecutors do not arbitrarily bring criminal charges. She points out that the prosecutor's job is to see justice done by presenting the best case to prove guilt, or if they find evidence of innocence, by disclosing it and freeing the accused. Bass maintains that most prosecutors do not abuse the system and if one does, appropriate sanctions and state bar associations would punish the prosecutor. Bass is the director of legal publications for the California District Attorneys Association in Sacramento, California.

As you read, consider the following questions:

1. Why do prosecutors bring charges, according to the author?
2. How are charges referred to the prosecutor's office, according to Bass?
3. Some prosecutors have been known to hide information to get a conviction. Why does Bass oppose reversing these convictions?

Brigitte A. Bass, "Prosecutorial Standards," a paper revised by the author in October 1992 for inclusion in the present volume.

Prosecutors, school teachers, ministers, and doctors all have been entrusted with the responsibility of serving the public. Most have diligently and ethically fulfilled their roles. Some have engaged in dishonest and illegal behavior. The media focuses upon those few who fall into the latter category.

Does the fact that a handful of individuals fail to carry out their responsibilities justify labeling an entire profession corrupt and untrustworthy? Most critical thinkers would concede the answer is not to condemn the innocent along with the guilty because to do so would be neglecting to look at the real issue.

Every profession has standards or a code of ethics by which those who practice in the area are expected to abide. In the case of prosecutors, the standards are high and rigorously enforced. The purpose of this article is to educate readers on these standards that govern prosecutors in crime charging and disclosure of information to the defense.

The Prosecution's Job

Prosecutors are entrusted with the responsibility of representing the interests of the People—all the People. They act on behalf of everyone and not on behalf of individual victims, witnesses, or even their own electorates.

Prosecutors bring charges because citizens and legislators have passed laws to:

1) Protect themselves and their property from dangerous individuals;

2) Deter individuals from committing crime; and

3) Punish individuals for disobeying laws on which the preservation of an orderly and free society rests.

Generally, prosecutors are not the initiating force in crime charging. Typically, victims and witnesses report crimes to law enforcement agencies such as the police department or sheriff's office. These agencies investigate such reports to identify and refer cases for prosecution. Within the prosecutor's office a matrix of responsibilities and internal oversight is utilized in evaluating whether charges should be brought.

Depending upon jurisdictional population and funding resources, a prosecutor's office may employ a few or several hundred prosecutors. Each prosecutor does not have unfettered discretion to bring charges. Typically, an internal review process is utilized whereby designated prosecutors with extensive experience evaluate cases to finalize the charging process. That is, they determine if and what cases should be brought by the office. Special categories of alleged cases, such as career crime, organized crime or consumer fraud cases may be referred to individual units for either initial intake or final decision.

Prosecutors within those special units may again, but often do so for the first time, review the cases and determine whether charges should be brought.

Percentage of Prosecutions

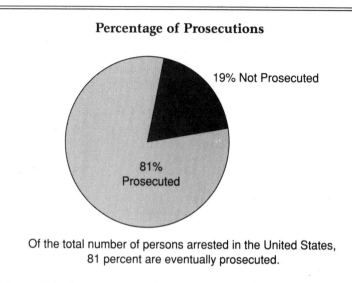

19% Not Prosecuted

81% Prosecuted

Of the total number of persons arrested in the United States, 81 percent are eventually prosecuted.

Source: Federal Bureau of Investigation, *Sourcebook of Criminal Justice, Criminal Justice Statistics*, 1991.

For various reasons, a prosecutor may decide not to bring charges. First, a prosecutor has a legal and ethical obligation entirely separate from the obligation to prosecute crimes. That obligation is to protect the innocent. Second, although an individual may be factually guilty, there may exist evidence which is factually insufficient, or for various statutory or constitutional reasons is not admissible in trial.

A prosecutor should bring charges only if:

1. Based upon a complete investigation and consideration of all available information (the prosecutor may have to get evidence that is unavailable by search warrant or subpoena), the prosecutor believes, in good faith, the evidence shows the accused is guilty of the crime to be charged;

2. There is legally sufficient, admissible evidence of a corpus delicti;

3. There is legally sufficient, admissible evidence of the accused's identity as the perpetrator of the crime charged; and

4. The admissible evidence is of such a convincing force that it would warrant conviction of the crime charged by a reason-

165

able and objective fact-finder after hearing the most plausible defense that could be raised in light of the evidence.

The prosecutor has the responsibility to select and file a charge or charges that adequately describe the offense or offenses committed by the accused and provide for an adequate sentence under the facts known to the prosecutor at the time of charging. The prosecutor should select and file an alternative charge or charges to describe, more correctly, the offense or offenses allegedly committed, as long as prospective punishment levels under the alternative charges are approximately the same.

The prosecutor should not use the charging process to obtain leverage to induce a guilty plea to a lesser charge prior to trial. There should be a reasonable expectation of conviction on the designated charge. In some jurisdictions, if after a trial or mistrial a prosecutor adds to the charges against a defendant, the prosecutor must establish that the new or additional charge is justified by an objective change in circumstances that could not have been discovered originally.

Even if the arresting agency and prosecutor are satisfied that the charges are supported by probable cause, an independent judge still has to be persuaded the charges are justified. If, after the institution of criminal charges, the prosecutor responsible for prosecuting the charges becomes aware those charges are not supported by probable cause, he or she is required to promptly advise the court in which the criminal matter is pending.

Disclosure of Evidence

Prosecutors must make timely and complete disclosure of relevant information to the defense. Constitutional due process mandates that a prosecutor never thwart defense efforts to obtain relevant evidence or other information. There is also a duty to correct misinformation. Drastic sanctions may be imposed for failure to disclose or correct data essential to the defense.

Neither the defense nor the prosecution is required to disclose certain types of confidential information protected constitutionally or statutorily. However, other than in these exceptions, a prosecutor ordinarily has no interest in withholding information from the defense. To do otherwise would be contrary to the prosecutor's obligation to afford an accused a fair trial.

Certainly there are isolated cases in which individual prosecutors have violated disclosure standards. However, it would not be prudent to advocate that reversals should be required for all convictions in which a prosecutor has failed to disclose information. The courts should review the error and determine its magnitude and whether it was harmful. If it was harmful the conviction should be reversed. Any judge who sees misconduct by any lawyer should refer the conduct to the state bar association.

Appropriate sanctions and punishment should be brought against the prosecutor by the courts and state bar associations. Additionally, an elected prosecutor may be impeached or removed by an "Accusation" as well as removed by popular defeat at the electoral polls. Moreover, elected prosecutors are expected to exert conscious oversight of their staffs to discipline appropriately anyone who violates legal, constitutional or office standards or canons of ethics.

Abuse Is Not Rampant

Abuse of power does occur. However, the existence of isolated incidents does not warrant adopting the viewpoint that such occurrences are rampant. Excessive and irresponsible use of rhetoric without adequate basis is not performing a public service. Sensationalism does not teach students how to reach an argumentative conclusion based upon critical thought and analysis.

A complex matrix of accountability does exist within the criminal justice system. Additionally, all members of the bar are ethically obligated to report known violations. Any lawyer who pontificates about the rampant ethical violations of prosecutors ought to footnote the number of times he or she has reported to the appropriate authorities alleged violations of his or her colleagues.

Recognizing Statements That Are Provable

We are constantly confronted with statements and generalizations about social and moral problems. In order to think clearly about these problems, it is useful if one can make a basic distinction between statements for which evidence can be found and other statements that cannot be verified or proved because evidence is not available or the issue is so controversial that it cannot be definitely proved.

Readers should be aware that magazines, newspapers, and other sources often contain statements of a controversial nature. The following activity is designed to allow experimentation with statements that are provable and those that are not.

The following statements are taken from the viewpoints in this chapter. Consider each statement carefully. *Mark P for any statement you believe is provable. Mark U for any statement you feel is unprovable because of the lack of evidence. Mark C for any statement you think is too controversial to be proved to everyone's satisfaction.*

If you are doing this activity as a member of a class or group, compare your answers with those of other class or group members. Be able to defend your answers. You may discover that others come to different conclusions than you do. Listening to the reasons others present for their answers may give you valuable insights into recognizing statements that are provable.

P = provable
U = unprovable
C = too controversial

168

1. Everyone, guilty or innocent, is entitled to a fair trial.

2. Lawyers who defend the guilty are without conscience.

3. Many lawyers believe that the criminal justice system is un-ethical and corrupt.

4. Procedural, prosecutorial, and judicial misconduct is widespread in the criminal justice system.

5. The injustices inflicted on the guilty by the criminal justice system outweigh the harm done to victims.

6. The courts foster the attitude that violent criminals can get away with heinous crimes without fear of punishment.

7. The Texas State Bar's criminal justice section has lost 25 percent of its fifteen hundred members since 1986.

8. All of the attorneys who left public defense in Texas during the 1986 to 1991 period were disillusioned by the system.

9. Criminal defense law is the least profitable of all the types of law practice.

10. The prosecutor decides whether to bring criminal charges, what charges to bring, and whom to charge.

11. Prosecutors wield awesome power within the criminal justice system and many prosecutors abuse that power.

12. Many prosecutors choose to prosecute certain individuals based on race, sex, or religion, and not on the weight of the evidence against these people.

13. Prosecutors often obtain evidence that proves that a defendant is innocent.

14. The media report cases of prosecutorial misconduct and ignore prosecutors who do their jobs honestly and proficiently.

15. Prosecutors are usually honest and professional.

16. Many attorneys and judges complain about ethical violations within the system, but few have reported these violations.

17. The criminal justice system in the United States may have problems but it is still the best one.

18. Lawyers persuade their clients that their problems can be solved through lawsuits.

Periodical Bibliography

The following articles have been selected to supplement the diverse views presented in this chapter.

William T. Braithwaite — "Hearts and Minds," *ABA Journal*, September 1990. Available from 750 N. Lake Shore Dr., Chicago, IL 60611.

Sam Benson — "Why I Quit Practicing Law," *Newsweek*, November 4, 1991.

Margaret Carlson, James Carney, and Jerome Cramer — "Highly Public Prosecutors," *Time*, February 5, 1990.

Robert F. Drinan — "The Flowering of Legal Ethics in America," *America*, August 19, 1989.

Linda Greenhouse — "Can Lawyers Be Forced to Represent the Poor?" *The New York Times*, March 3, 1989.

Jet — "Cook County, IL Gets First Woman Public Defender," March 23, 1992.

Richard Lacayo — "You Don't Always Get Perry Mason," *Time*, June 1, 1992.

Neil A. Lewis — "Drug Lawyers' Quandary: Lure of Money vs. Ethics," *The New York Times*, February 9, 1990.

Barbara K. Maddux — "Presumed Innocent," *Life*, special issue, Fall 1991.

Laura Mansnerus — "For Lawyers, Crime May Not Pay," *The New York Times*, December 17, 1989.

Eric Pooley — "Reality 101," *New York*, October 21, 1991.

Paul Craig Roberts — "Maybe They Should Call It the Injustice Department," *Business Week*, June 16, 1991.

Morton Stavis — "New Order in the Courts," *The Nation*, July 6, 1992.

Stuart Taylor — "The 'Judicial Activists' Are Always on the Other Side," *The New York Times*, July 3, 1988.

Stuart Taylor — "When Is Justice a Bargain and When Isn't It?" *The New York Times*, March 21, 1986.

Do Police Abuse
Their Authority?

CRIMINAL
JUSTICE

Chapter Preface

On March 3, 1991, four Los Angeles police officers beat motorist Rodney King after he had led them on a high-speed chase. The officers who beat King said he was an overpowering, drug-crazed man who resisted arrest. The incident might have been brushed aside and never heard about, except that a local resident videotaped the arrest. The video showed the police beating King while he was on the ground unarmed, handcuffed, and not resisting arrest. King suffered multiple fractures, internal injuries, and brain damage. The video shocked and horrified viewers around the world. Yet, jurors at the trial for the four officers accused of beating King acquitted the men of police brutality.

This trial reflects how perceptions of police abuse vary. In the eighty-one seconds of videotape shown on television, the public saw King clubbed and kicked fifty-six times. They perceived that the officers were out of control, abusing their authority to maintain law and order.

The jury members, however, were influenced not only by the shocking violence of the video but by hours of testimony in the courtroom. They listened as defense attorneys discussed each action recorded on the video, asserting that the officers followed acceptable police procedures and conduct to subdue King. In the end, the jury perceived that four frightened officers had acted within their rights in aggressively subduing a belligerent criminal.

The divergent views of the jurors and the public in the King case reveal the difficulty in determining when police action is appropriate aggression and when it is brutality. Society expects police officers to fight crime and permits officers to use force to do so. Many people, however, are shocked when they see police using force—especially when it seems excessive. Police, on the other hand, say the public is ignorant about the conditions under which police officers work. Daily they face life-threatening conditions, confronting criminals in order to maintain peace in society. Occasionally this means police must use aggressive force to stop crime.

Clearly, what one person views as police misconduct, another might view as legitimate police authority. The authors of the following viewpoints discuss these conflicting perceptions of police actions.

"Police regularly utilize . . . varying levels of abuse, threat, and torture to extract confessions and demonstrate police effectiveness in fighting crime. "

Police Violence Is Excessive

Kerwin Brook

Police abuse their power and authority by disregarding the rights of minorities, according to Kerwin Brook. In the following viewpoint, Brook argues that police harass minorities and the poor by using unnecessary violent force to arrest them and attack innocent citizens when the police arbitrarily perceive some of these people as a threat. The author contends that the conservative Supreme Court and conservative political climate have allowed police to abuse their authority to protect white Americans. Brook, a free-lance writer, is a contributor to *Z Magazine*, a monthly leftist magazine.

As you read, consider the following questions:

1. Why are there few tapings and videos of police violence, according to Brook?
2. How has the U.S. Supreme Court promoted police abuse, according to the author?
3. Why are minority policemen sometimes more violent than white officers, according to Brook?

Kerwin Brook, "Baddest Gang," *Z Magazine*, July/August 1991. Reprinted with permission.

For years the mainstream press has ignored or minimized the problem of police violence. Non-white communities have meanwhile continued to suffer widespread brutality that often parallels that found in many underdeveloped countries. While the videotaped beating of Rodney King on March 3, 1989, has raised some much needed critical attention, there have been a number of tapings of police brutality over the past several years, many in the Los Angeles area, and all involving victims of color. In 1989, a television crew filmed Long Beach police as they arrested off-duty Black police officer, Don Jackson, at a traffic stop. The film shows the officers cursing at Jackson and then shoving his head through a nearby store window. In April 1988, a security guard filmed a Sacramento deputy as he pulled a gun and placed it under the chin of a non-resisting Black man he had pulled over. The following month San Bernardino police were filmed as they brutally clubbed five Latinos while responding to a noise complaint. Cerritos police were videotaped while beating several Samoans during a bridal shower in February 1989. Other tapings include New York's Tompkins Square "Riot" where police with taped-over badges beat and clubbed numerous people in order to enforce a curfew, and the May 1989 beatings and dog attacks on Black students in Virginia Beach during annual Springfest activities.

Police Brutality Exists

There would be more photos and videos of police violence, but typically those who stop to watch incidents of brutality are arrested and beaten up themselves. In August 1990, Chicago police beat a Latino man who refused to leave his window while another man was being roughed up. The officers broke down the man's door, hit him several times, and threw him down the stairs before charging him with resisting arrest. In another case, a West Virginia editor found a cross burning on his lawn after publishing several articles on a brutality case. Given the levels of violence available to the police, and the frequent futility of filing charges, it is amazing that anyone has the courage or perseverance to do so. Despite this, a number of cases have surfaced over the past several years:

- CHICAGO, IL—FEBRUARY 1982: After two anti-gang officers were killed in a Black neighborhood, police went on a two-week rampage, systematically invading every apartment on the block of the shooting. In order to obtain information, police shoved guns in people's mouths, placed plastic bags over their heads, and used an electric torture device similar to that used by U.S. military interrogators in Vietnam. Police finally obtained a confession from Andrew Wilson after shocking him numerous times and placing his body against a radiator inflicting second degree burns. Jon

Burge, who was in charge of the operation, has since been promoted to Commander (*Chicago Lawyer*).

- NEW YORK, NY—APRIL 1985: In order to extract confessions on drug charges, police beat and then used a stun gun as a torture device on four different suspects. One of the victims had his head slammed into a wall repeatedly and was then shocked 43 times until finally agreeing to falsely accuse himself of selling $10 worth of marijuana to an undercover cop. No officers in the station house responded to either the screams or the racial slurs which were hurled at Black and Latino suspects (*New York Times*).

- HEMPHILL, TX—DECEMBER 1987: After being arrested on false charges of drunk driving and public intoxication, Loyal Garner and two other Blacks were thrown into a detox cell. After the three began banging on their cell door demanding to make a phone call, the sheriff entered the cell and hit Garner five or six times while a deputy stood by with his hand on his gun. Garner was then taken from his cell and beaten to death (*New York Times*).

- LOS ANGELES, CA—AUGUST 1988: In a raid supposedly intended to recover drugs and weapons used by gang mem-

Public Perception of Police Brutality

Q. When you hear charges of police brutality, how likely do you think it is that the charges are justified?

Percent who say the charges are justified:

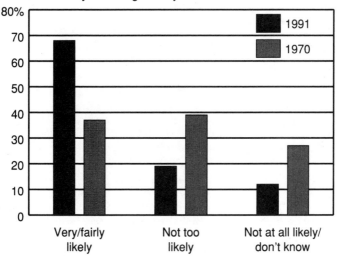

Source: CBS/*New York Times* poll, April 4, 1991.

bers, over 70 officers descended on four apartment buildings at 30th and Dalton. Police tore through the building with axes, destroying appliances, furniture, stairs, rendering the buildings uninhabitable. While only seven residents were arrested, dozens were injured as police kicked people in the ribs and groin, hit them with heavy metal flashlights, and used choke holds, all while having them handcuffed. Police left after spray painting anti-gang graffiti including "LAPD Rules." Five ounces of pot and a quarter gram of crack cocaine were seized (*LA Times*).

- MIAMI, FL—JANUARY 1989: Clement Lloyd, also Black, was fatally shot in the head by Miami officer William Lozano. Lloyd was fleeing on motorcycle after another officer had tried to pull him over speeding. Lozano, standing a few blocks away, entered the street as the motorcycle approached and fired as Lloyd passed. A passenger on the bike died the following day of head injuries sustained during the subsequent crash. Riots ensued (*Newsweek*).

- CHICAGO, IL—AUGUST 1989: Two Black teenagers, Joseph Weaver and Calvin McLynn, were picked up by white police officers after a White Sox game. The boys were driven around by the officers, racially insulted, and then physically assaulted before being dropped off in a notoriously racist neighborhood near a white gang. The boys were chased by the gang until McLynn was caught and beaten unconscious (*Chicago Sun-Times*).

- ITTA BENA, MS—SEPTEMBER 1989: After a high school football game, Darrell and Martin Wilson, both Black, got into an argument with a group of whites. After being told of the incident, police dragged them off a bus, and took them to the police station where they were severely beaten and tortured. After hitting and kicking them, police used an electric cattle prod which they placed on Darrell and Martin's genitals (*Jackson Advocate*).

- TEANECK, NJ—APRIL 1990: Officers shot and killed 15-year-old Philip Pannell, Jr. Pannell, who is Black, had been running away from two white police officers and had yelled "Don't shoot!" before being shot in the back. An independent pathologist confirmed witness reports that his hands were in the air when shot (*Village Voice*).

- JACKSON, MS—APRIL 1990: Johnny Griffin, 37 and Black, was killed in cold blood by two police officers. A man who was with Griffin at the time was forced to stand behind a tree so he would be unable to see anything. A second witness attests that Griffin had already dropped a gun retrieved earlier to ward off a local gang. Officers fired two shots at Griffin who had been standing passively with his hands in the air (*Jackson Advocate*).

These cases represent only a fraction of the more extreme

cases. They say nothing about the brutality poor and especially non-white people suffer on a routine basis. Beatings like that of Rodney King, where suspects are handcuffed and then systematically punched, kicked, clubbed, shocked with a stun gun, or set upon by a police dog, are common. Beatings of lesser severity, where only a few bruises are sustained or a few teeth knocked out, are so common as to be practically matters of course in many locales. Police regularly utilize "the third degree," i.e. varying levels of abuse, threat, and torture to extract confessions and demonstrate police effectiveness in fighting crime. Gang members are frequently dropped off in a rival gang's territory to punish them. Being stopped, thrown up against a wall, and held without bail for days or even months is a common experience for many people of color. Police shootings of non-whites are also a relatively common occurrence. During the weekend before writing this article, unarmed men of color were shot in Chicago, Houston, and Washington, DC. Mitchell Kennard in Houston died after he "appeared to reach for a weapon" while driving away. In Washington, riots erupted after Daniel Gomez was shot, apparently while handcuffed. This is the *reality* of a police state which already exists in many communities of color. This is the reality which, more than any other factor, leads to riots.

Racist Police Policies

Having Ronald Reagan and George Bush in power for over a decade certainly hasn't helped. In what was a deliberate attempt at racist manipulation, Bush used Willie Horton as a propaganda tool against Michael Dukakis. Bush chose Horton, a Black man who had raped and killed a white woman, to invoke racist fears and prejudices about crime. Racist bias overrode the fact that in the overwhelming majority of rape and other crimes, the perpetrator and victim are of the same race.

Bush has followed up this racist campaign with racist policies. Over $44 billion a year is spent on police and prisons in the U.S., already the most highly incarcerated population in the world. Currently the U.S. proportionately imprisons more than twice the number of Blacks than does South Africa. Police and prison expenditures have increased four times faster than money spent on education, and twice as fast as monies spent for health care. In his first year as president, Bush spent $10 billion for the "war on drugs" alone, paying for this directly with cuts to economic development programs and public housing subsidies.

Supreme Court decisions passed by Reagan and Bush appointees have also had an impact. Over the past few years, the Court has restricted Miranda rights against self-incrimination, made it easier to use illegally obtained evidence in court, eased standards of police brutality, and most recently made it legal to use coerced confessions during trial. Police have been using such tactics against non-whites for years. The Court legalized what was already more or less standard operating procedure.

Another factor which creates problems is the way most police departments are allowed to investigate themselves. After the 1982 rampage in Chicago, nearly 200 complaints of excessive force were filed with the police department's Office of Professional Standards. The OPS "lost" 130 of these complaints. Even where civilian review boards exist, they are often just public relation tools with little independence or actual power to investigate charges and discipline officers.

Only 2 Percent Prosecuted

In view of the rapidly escalating police brutality and other misconduct since the 1980s (justified by the "war on drugs and crime"), the only thing that's surprising are the exclamations of disbelief emanating from all sides of the political and social spectrum.

This brutality is nothing new, and it's routine for police to lie about it and conspire to cover for each other in "the brotherhood." The Justice Department receives some 2,500 criminal civil-rights complaints per year; 90 percent involve police misconduct. Only 2 percent are ever prosecuted.

In most major cities, police are breaking down doors without search warrants, stopping and searching anyone they choose on the sidewalk or street, harassing and arresting young people for wearing "gang colors" or for "drug loitering," threatening and abusing anyone who questions them, and refusing to supply their badge numbers upon request. Cases of fiendish police behavior happen daily in the ghetto areas of every city in America.

Barbara Dority, *The Humanist*, July/August 1991.

Of course Bush, the Supreme Court, and the OPS are more the symptoms than the actual causes. Structural explanations revolve around two separate but related causes: racism and domestic colonization. Unlike other types of crime, the vast majority of police brutality cases are committed by white police officers against non-white victims. In almost all of these cases, racial epithets are part of the verbal onslaught victims suffer. Oftentimes members of the police department are actually members of the KKK. Other times officers are simply expressing the latent racism conditioned day in and day out by the countless images of non-white criminals throughout the media.

Attacks such as that in Itta Bena typify cases where police officers really are "klan members without the hood."

Victims of Police Oppression

But with the increased hiring of non-whites by police departments, a number of cases have surfaced in which Black officers have participated in attacks on other Blacks, and Latino officers have attacked other Latinos. On many Native reservations, police brutality is almost as big a problem as in many white dominated rural areas. Non-white officers are often even more violent than white officers as they attempt to demonstrate their "toughness" against others of the same race. "Simple" racism is not the whole story.

Communities of color occupy a quasi-colonial status in the U.S. As oppressed nationalities, peoples of color have their culture oppressed and labor exploited. American Indian Movement (AIM) activist, Ward Churchill, notes that even when laws are administered by the subject populations, they are created by and serve the interests of power. Increasingly the police are seen by people of color as an occupying army whose role is to protect property rights rather than people, and to enforce order against oppressed groups. The police often harass people of color in order to create a feeling of safety in predominantly white-owned business and residential areas. Anyone who has an "attitude problem," or who fails to demonstrate total subservience, is subject to beating and imprisonment. Men of color are more directly targeted than women because in racist/sexist imagination they represent a greater "threat to the peace." The day-to-day operations of the police blend into the more overtly political harassment suffered by groups such as the Black Panthers, the Brown Berets, and AIM.

Growing up as a white in suburbia, and then moving to predominantly-white Boulder, Colorado, it was too easy to remain unaware of these realities. Being an activist for a number of years has done all too little to change my awareness. None of the left-wing magazines I read regularly address the topic of police brutality. How is it that when the NAACP made police brutality their number one issue in July 1990, I never heard about it? On an issue which should be on everyone's mind as much as torture in El Salvador or the destruction of the Amazon rainforests, why aren't left publications devoting regular coverage? Police brutality occurs against other oppressed groups, notably lesbians/gays and the homeless, but this also receives far too little attention within the mainstream left. What exactly *are* we representing if we fail to address these gaps in our own priorities?

"Force is sometimes needed to compel obedience to the law."

Police Violence Is Sometimes Justifiable

Stacey C. Koon

On March 3, 1991, four Los Angeles policemen were videotaped beating Rodney King into submission before arresting him. The tape was picked up by a local television station and shown throughout the world. It caused a public outrage and cast suspicion on the entire Los Angeles police department. In the following viewpoint, Stacey C. Koon, a sergeant who commanded the officers who beat King, argues that sometimes violent force is justifiable. He contends that physical violence becomes necessary when no other alternative is given to police to subdue a dangerous and life-threatening suspect. Koon has been a police officer with the Los Angeles Police Department since 1976.

As you read, consider the following questions:

1. Why is an impulsive cop just as dangerous as a suspect high on drugs, according to Koon?
2. What was the real reason for the Rodney King incident, according to the author?
3. What three alternatives does Koon suggest could have been used by the Los Angeles police to subdue King?

Police work is often violent, often brutal. It's not pretty, but that's the way it is. That's the way it has been throughout history.

You see, I am not just an unwilling practitioner of the use of force to command obedience to the law. Using force is not simply a matter of following the policies and procedures required by the Los Angeles Police Department. I learned this while I was delving into the philosophical basis for the work I did as a street cop. That was in 1978 while I was pursuing a master's degree in criminal justice at Cal State University in Los Angeles, where I had received a bachelor's degree in that field four years earlier. The topic of my criminal justice master's thesis was a history of police organizations and how they have operated throughout the ages to enforce the rules that society imposes upon itself for structured, civilized interaction.

Understanding King's Arrest

Police organizations have undergone many transformations throughout the centuries. In primitive societies, police functions were performed by hunters or priests. Then, as societies became more civilized and more complex, police work became more structured, with the society's military arm, the army or militia, usually assigned the task of civilian control. The modern era of police work, which you can date to about the late eighteenth century, saw the development of professional police organizations. Today, cops have an ever-widening array of sophisticated tools available to help them command civil order—tools such as vehicular on-board portable computers designed to speed communications, and advanced scientific techniques, like genetic analysis, to aid in the solution of crimes.

But throughout human history, one element of police work has remained relatively unchanged. It is this:

Force is sometimes needed to compel obedience to the law. In a perfect society, reason would replace force. But we are imperfect humans. So, occasionally, it is necessary to use force on somebody intent upon endangering or harming himself or other people.

Still, the use of force by police officers has become more civilized over the years. That's the way it should be. In the old days bad guys got shot because they were bad. But it's more complicated than that. Today good people can get screwed up on drugs, but that doesn't mean you have to kill them. It means you must try to keep them from hurting themselves or others. Quick-draw sheriffs might have been needed in the Old West, but in law enforcement on today's city streets an impulsive cop is almost as dangerous as a dusted felon.

For this reason, modern police departments have rigid policies on when to use force and how to use it. The policies have become tighter as minority groups have become more vocal, and justifiably so, in urging restraints to prevent abuse of police powers that so frequently characterized the use of official force in days past.

Police Anguish over Use of Violence

In the first course I ever taught in ethics for police in 1975, one of my police-officer students said to me, "You know, Mr. Delattre, most cops don't like to hurt people." In the years since, I have learned how right he was.

I have seen police officers injured because they limited their use of force against wildly violent individuals, and I have seen them refrain from using deadly force even in life-threatening situations. Many police feel anguish after using fully justified force; few take pleasure in it, let alone react with glee. Some of my police friends have been shot in the line of duty. It is only a matter of fortune that none of them is among the 1,514 American police who were killed feloniously or died in the line of duty between 1980 and 1989 or the many who have been killed since.

Even so, most police around the country do not have a bunker mentality. They go on forces knowing what they'll have to put up with; they like their jobs and are ready and able to stand the pressure.

Edwin J. Delattre, *The Washington Post National Weekly Edition*, April 8-14, 1991.

These are important concepts to understand in the context of Rodney King's arrest. This is because a decade ago the city of Los Angeles overreacted to minority demands on limiting force, and thereby restricted an officer's ability to subdue a suspect. Limitations on using force are fine, but they necessarily mean that cops must use other legal means when force is necessary. . . .

You see, Rodney King forced us to dig as deeply into our bag of tricks as we could reach. We began with the first level of force: physical presence. You can't get much more physically present than four squad cars, lights flashing and sirens blaring, a police helicopter hovering directly overhead, its spotlight shining on the scene, and officers crouching behind their doors with guns drawn. That's industrial-strength physical presence. But it didn't have any effect on Rodney King.

So we escalated to the next use of force: verbalization. We verbalized Rodney King so much that he would have been bored if he hadn't been intoxicated. In just eighty-two seconds of videotape he got fourteen commands to get down in a felony prone position—on his belly, face in the dirt, hands behind his back.

And this doesn't count the commands given before the video-tape began, the orders to King by Officers Tim Singer and Melanie Singer and various LAPD patrolmen to get out of the car and down on his stomach.

Verbalization had no more impact on Rodney King than our physical presence. So I ratcheted the use of force up a notch. That's when I ordered the swarm. Ordinarily a swarm will end a confrontation and result in a suspect on the ground and cuffed up behind his back. But not Rodney King. He tossed four officers off his arms and legs like they were irritating insects, rather than armed, well-trained professional police officers. He was stronger than four street cops.

Now the use of force is getting serious. That's when I zap him with the TASER. Twice. A total of one hundred thousand volts in fifty thousand-volt increments. It put Rodney King to his knees, and eventually put him down. But he came right back up and charged Officer Lawrence Powell.

The use-of-force cupboard is getting bare now. There's only the use of PR 24 metal batons between the TASER and deadly force—a gun or the chokehold. So we go to the baton. And here, too, we escalate and de-escalate the violence. Officers Timothy Wind and Powell used their batons in a measured way, moving in to strike the suspect two or three times, then stepping back to evaluate his response. If he's still, the beating is halted. It begins again only when Rodney King's on the rise and threatening another assault on the officers. Which Rodney King does, repeatedly.

Limited Vision

The customary use of batons, striking the body mass, isn't working. So the decision must be made: Do we go to deadly force? A gun or a chokehold? Has the baton been exhausted? No. Not yet. I decide that a chokehold is especially ruled out, because chokeholds have been associated with the death of blacks. Rodney King is black. We'll be in a world of trouble if we use a chokehold, even if it's routine and doesn't cause any permanent damage. And we sure don't want to kill him. So let's ratchet the violence up only half a notch here, let's use the baton on his joints and see if the higher level of pain can force compliance. So we begin power-stroking the knees, the elbows, the ankles.

Finally, it works. Rodney King submits. The incident has been violent. It's been brutal. It's been ugly. But it's been necessary under LAPD rules. . . .

The point is, other devices and techniques are used by police in other large cities to avoid the type of violence employed on Rodney King, but the LAPD hasn't adopted them. Why? Because the Los Angeles Police Department believes its own propaganda. The LAPD believes it is the best in the world. The department is constantly told it is the best by its officials. LA coppers read about how great they are in newspapers, in books such as Joseph Wambaugh's *New Centurions*, in intradepartmental communications, and on such popular television shows as "Dragnet" and "One-Adam-12." From the moment you enter the LAPD academy, you're taught that you are the elite of the law enforcement community. You're the best of the best. . . .

When you think you're the best of the best, though, you can become convinced that your ideas are the only ones that count. It's dangerous when you start to believe your own propaganda.

And that is one explanation why the LAPD has steadfastly refused to acquire other use-of-force appliances that would provide a cushion between using the baton to thump a suspect into submission or drawing your gun and pulling the trigger.

And what are some of the devices used in other modern police departments? Well, one goes back to antiquity. It's a net, a simple net that's thrown over a suspect so he or she can be pulled to the ground and cuffed without further injury to the suspect or danger to the arresting officers. The Romans used nets, but not the LAPD.

Another, more modern device is a Velcro blanket. It works somewhat like the net. Officers surround a suspect and wrap him in the blanket, securing it by merely pushing the velcro outside panels together. The suspect is immobilized within the confining blanket. It's as simple as a straightjacket, and much easier to put on.

Then there's the "leg-grabber." Have you ever seen the device used in supermarkets and other retail stores to twist light bulbs out of ceiling sockets? It's basically a gripper on the end of a long pole. Some smart cops adapted this for use with struggling suspects. The leg-grabber is a vise-like attachment on the end of an extended rod that permits the officer to grip a suspect's leg and bring him or her to the ground from a distance without tying up in a physical confrontation. Once the suspect is on the ground, he or she can be swarmed and cuffed by other officers.

So, you see, using a metal baton to beat Rodney King into submission wasn't the only tactic available if we had been somewhere other than Los Angeles. Neither was the TASER, chokehold, or gun.

The Rodney King incident was more than a brutal beating. It was, in truth, a serious indictment of the Los Angeles Police Department and its ability to control violence on the streets. Because, you see, force is an everyday affair for street cops in Los Angeles. An LA street cop who doesn't learn to live with violence doesn't live very long.

"Federal prosecution of law-enforcement officers who use excessive force often provides the only check on such unrestrained state power."

Federal Prosecution Would Help Punish Police Violence

Dirk Roggeveen

The Fourteenth Amendment states that no state shall deprive any person of life, liberty, or property without due process of law. This amendment gives the federal government the power to charge police with abuse when state or local governments are suspect of either ignoring or failing to uphold individual rights in police brutality cases, according to Dirk Roggeveen. In the following viewpoint, he argues that the federal government's authority sends a warning to police that they will be punished if they abuse their power. Roggeveen is a senior litigation attorney for the Institute for Justice in Washington, D.C.

As you read, consider the following questions:

1. When do federal authorities use Section 242, according to the author?
2. Why does Roggeveen believe that some prosecutions for state district attorneys are politically risky?
3. In the Arkansas case, what three things did the state prosecutor do that made federal authorities suspicious, according to the author?

Dirk Roggeveen, "Better Fed than Dead." Reprinted, with permission, from the August/September 1992 issue of *Reason* magazine. Copyright 1992 by the Reason Foundation, 3415 S. Sepulveda Blvd., Suite 400, Los Angeles, CA 90034.

The video images of Los Angeles police officers beating Rodney King in 1991 shocked the nation. Americans rarely have an opportunity to view, much less contemplate, the excessive use of state power by the police. Reactions to the officers' acquittal ranged from surprise to visceral anger, from stunned disbelief to the pyrotechnic.

I personally experienced the anger. By chance, I drove through South-Central Los Angeles several hours after the verdict. My car was attacked and badly damaged. Even as I escaped unharmed, I appreciated the irony of my predicament: I had spent the past five years prosecuting police-brutality cases for the Department of Justice. I was as disappointed as any at the jury's verdict.

Providing Equal Protection

Despite the department's pending investigation of the Rodney King beating, only after the state acquittal did the press and public become aware that the officers still faced federal prosecution. Some wondered why the Department of Justice hadn't acted sooner. Others, including some libertarians, asked why a federal prosecution did not constitute double jeopardy.

Chicago Tribune columnist Stephen Chapman, for instance, calls the federal prosecution "a trial mounted for political ends." Is this second trial taking place only because, as Chapman argues, George Bush "wants to look responsive to the black community"? Are we retrying the four officers because the jury didn't get it right the first time?

The Constitution indeed protects the Los Angeles Police Department [LAPD] officers from double jeopardy. But the federal government can independently prosecute a police-brutality case, even after an acquittal in a state court, for good reason. Residents of the United States are expected to obey both federal laws and the laws of the state in which they reside; the laws themselves, and the level of punishment meted out for breaking them, can differ.

State and local prosecutors also face pressures and incentives that can make it difficult to conduct a proper trial. And, most important, federal prosecution of criminal civil-rights violations helps ensure that everyone receives the equal protection of the law the Constitution guarantees—especially when that protection is denied by law-enforcement officers, who act as agents of the state.

Problems of Prosecuting

The Department of Justice had begun its own independent investigation of the Rodney King beating immediately after it occurred. The Federal Bureau of Investigation, the department's investigative arm, had been gathering evidence; prosecutors in the Criminal Section of the Civil Rights Division had been reviewing and evaluating that evidence. Had the state not prosecuted, federal action was inevitable.

Title 18 of the United States Code, Section 242, makes it a crime for any person who acts as an agent of the state intentionally to deprive an inhabitant of the United States of a right secured by the Constitution or any other federal, statutory law. This law was enacted in 1866 to enforce the 14th Amendment. Its purpose was to safeguard from abuses of state authority individual rights, including freedom from arrest and detention by unconstitutional methods, prohibitions against extorted confessions, and the right to a fair trial. Since state authorities had widely abused these individual protections, the statute was necessary at the time. It is just as necessary today.

Keeping Track of Abuses

Congress should give the Justice Department the power to intervene against systematic local abuses of constitutional rights. . . .

The federal government has the power to collect information on the number and type of citizen complaints against the police; on officers disciplined by departments and the nature of their offenses; on the number of officers prosecuted for local crimes; and on systems of review, command-control and accountability within local departments. If the government used that power, it might give us an idea how widespread police violence is, in what cities it is prevalent and what can be done to decrease it.

Paul Chevigny, *The Nation*, March 23, 1992.

Federal authorities use Section 242 to prosecute law-enforcement officers who use excessive force during an arrest. Under this section, in any given year, police officers are convicted of everything from gratuitously striking to intentionally and wrongfully killing a suspect.

In the case of the LAPD officers, federal prosecutors properly remained on the sidelines until the jury in Simi Valley handed down its verdict. The Department of Justice seeks to preserve limited prosecutorial resources and defers to the principles of federalism whenever states decide to prosecute. Any time an officer is convicted and receives a sentence commensurate with the crime, no federal prosecution will follow. Thus the Criminal Section can direct its own resources at those crimes which might otherwise go unpunished.

Ideally, local criminal-justice authorities would prosecute all crimes at the state level, including those committed by local police. Yet such prosecutions are often politically risky for local prosecutors, who are, after all, elected officials. The public perceives the police as the "thin blue line" that protects law-abiding citizens from vicious criminals. Any time police officers are prosecuted, critics accuse the prosecutors of coddling criminals.

Additionally, by the very nature of their work, local prosecutors must depend on and work closely with the police. It is hardly surprising that local officials might wish to find any excuse to avoid prosecuting police-brutality cases. If the Department of Justice always prosecuted first, regardless of any state prosecution, it would provide an easy excuse for local authorities to do nothing about police brutality.

Deciding to Make a Federal Case

When local authorities try but fail to adequately prosecute and punish law-enforcement officers for civil-rights violations, the Department of Justice must then decide whether to pursue a federal case. The department has established guidelines that govern when a federal prosecution may follow a state trial. Before federal prosecutors may seek an indictment, the case must satisfy two conditions: Further prosecution must satisfy an unvindicated federal interest; and the federal prosecution must be likely to succeed.

The outcome of the local trial may determine if there is an unvindicated federal interest. For example, a local jury may vote to acquit on state charges despite overwhelming evidence that federal law was violated. The LAPD acquittals may satisfy this condition.

After an acquittal in state court, federal prosecutors must then determine how likely they are to succeed in a second trial. If the state prosecutors proceeded in good faith before an unbiased trial court that admitted the appropriate evidence, an acquittal may indicate that the jury honestly harbored reasonable doubt. In such instances, it's hard to see what difference it makes whether the case was tried in federal or state court. The guidelines sensibly prohibit a "let's try it and see" approach.

Often, however, peculiarities in a state trial may lead to an acquittal; subsequent federal prosecution would likely result in conviction. For example, federal jury pools are drawn from federal judicial districts, which are often more ethnically and demographically diverse than state pools. If in a state trial jurors were excluded solely because of their race, retrial by a federal court may be appropriate. Other considerations have included the different rules of evidence in federal trials, additional evidence available to federal prosecutors, and flawed trial tactics or weak prosecutions by local authorities. Any of these factors may enter the Department of Justice's analysis of the Simi Valley verdict.

Independent Federal Enforcement

It is also important to recognize that not all state prosecutions of police officers are conducted competently, legitimately, and in good faith. In 1990, for instance, an elected county prosecutor in Arkansas charged the county sheriff with assault only after it became apparent that, despite local efforts to thwart the investigation, the Department of Justice intended to prosecute him for beating a suspect in his custody. Upon reviewing the trial, federal prosecutors became suspicious of the local prosecution: The prosecutor had not subpoenaed essential witnesses, had ignored entire lines of evidence, and had presented unconvincing arguments for conviction. To no one's surprise, the jury voted to acquit.

Establishing Guidelines to Curb Abuse

Although existing aid programs explicitly forbid "direction, supervision or control" by any federal official over local police, the National Institute of Justice is authorized to conduct research on and make suggestions for the improvement of the criminal justice system. The Bureau of Justice Assistance provides funds to local police for equipment and to assist specific programs, such as drug enforcement. If the federal government possessed adequate information about police violence, it could establish guidelines on the use of non-lethal weapons, on adequate command responsibility and on fair review of complaints of police brutality. These could legitimately be disseminated to local departments, just as the Justice Department now gives advice and funds for law enforcement against drug trafficking and money laundering.

Paul Chevigny, *The Nation*, March 23, 1992.

In such a case, to argue that "double jeopardy" should prevent the federal government from conducting an independent prosecution is to argue for a system that allows local corruption to successfully thwart justice. It is to argue for a system where an American's constitutional right to be free from the abuse of state authority is secured only by that same authority. The federal jury convicted the Arkansas sheriff and he was sentenced to prison.

Even when the local jury convicts, unvindicated federal interests can remain. State judges often give convicted police officers light sentences. Some of these punishments are legitimate; others aren't. By contrast, federal convictions for civil-rights offenses can lead to prison sentences of many years and fines totaling thousands of dollars. When law officers violate civil rights, probation, suspended sentences, or even minimal jail time may not constitute a sufficient punishment or deterrent.

Not too long ago, a San Juan police officer was convicted of aggravated assault by the Commonwealth of Puerto Rico. He had intentionally beaten an innocent pedestrian who was out for an evening stroll. The pedestrian died from the beating. The presiding judge fined the officer $500, and he was subsequently reinstated. Such a sentence sends a message to other officers that civil-rights violations are not serious offenses, even when those violations lead to the death of an innocent person. The officer was prosecuted in federal court, convicted of a felony, and sentenced to prison.

This example underscores the need for independent federal enforcement of civil-rights laws. The federal government must be able to secure constitutional rights to life and liberty, especially when local authorities fail to do so. Constitutional protections apply equally, whether you're in Louisiana, Los Angeles, or Alaska; these protections certainly include the right to be fairly tried before being subjected to severe punishment by agents of the state. Civil libertarians need to recognize that federal prosecution of law-enforcement officers who use excessive force often provides the only check on such unrestrained state power.

"Miranda *warnings as well as the exclusionary rule have been reported to be 'widely credited with improving professionalism among policemen.'*"

Civil Rights Protections Help Curb Police Violence

Christopher E. Smith

In the 1960s, the U.S. Supreme Court expanded the rights of criminal defendants in reaction to a history of police abuse and corruption. In the following viewpoint, Christopher E. Smith argues that as a result of these rights, police departments became more professional and police brutality decreased. He contends that the Supreme Court is now eroding these rights and therefore allowing police to return to their more violent tactics of curbing crime. Smith is a professor of political science at the University of Akron in Ohio.

As you read, consider the following questions:

1. What were two major rights recognized by the 1960s Supreme Court that helped police become more professional, according to Smith?
2. How is the Supreme Court in the 1990s different from the Court of the 1960s, according to the author?
3. What does Smith believe are two motivating factors that push police to test the boundaries of criminal defendants' rights?

From Christopher E. Smith, "Police Professionalism and the Rights of Criminal Defendants." Reprinted with permission from *Criminal Law Bulletin* 26 (2), © 1990 Research Institute of America, Inc., Warren Gorham Lamont Professional Publishing Division, 210 South St., Boston, MA 02111. All rights reserved.

During the 1980s, many of the U.S. Supreme Court's decisions on the constitutional rights of criminal defendants loosened restrictions on police behavior. Despite violations of Fourth Amendment search and seizure rules, the exclusionary rule has been limited to permit admission of evidence obtained through "good-faith" errors by police officers. In addition, the Court permitted police officers to question a suspect before informing him of his *Miranda* rights when the situation arguably posed a threat to "public safety." Although these and similar decisions reflect the changing composition of the Supreme Court, in particular the emerging dominance of Ronald Reagan appointees, the criminal procedure opinions are also rooted in perceptions about police professionalism.

Development of Police Professionalism

Historically, the police were a component of the prevailing political establishment. According to Sam Walker, they "enforced the narrow prejudices of their constituencies, harassing 'undesirables' or discouraging any kind of 'unwelcome' behavior." Becoming a law enforcement officer generally required few qualifications. Nearly any adult male could receive a badge and a gun if he were loyal to the controlling political interests in a particular city or town.

The risks of abusive behavior from politically motivated and untrained law enforcement officers were heightened by the absence of constitutional protections for criminal suspects. Early in U.S. constitutional history the Supreme Court had declared that the protections for individuals provided by the Bill of Rights, including the right to counsel, the right against self-incrimination, and the right to freedom from unreasonable search and seizure, applied only against the federal government. Although the Supreme Court slowly applied property rights and free speech rights against the states, the full application of criminal defendants' rights against the states did not occur until the 1960s. Thus during most of U.S. history police officers in many locales were relatively free to employ coercive and even violent methods against criminal defendants. . . .

The greatest judicial pressure for police reform and professionalization came with the controversial decisions defining criminal defendants' rights during the Warren era. For example, in the famous *Miranda v. Arizona* (1966) decision requiring police to inform suspects of their rights, Chief Justice Earl Warren devoted much of his opinion to a critique of abusive police practices. The decision provided relatively clear rules about what police must say to arrestees and clearly limited the potential for abusive interrogation practices. Similarly, *Mapp v. Ohio* (1961) provided relatively clear boundaries for police behavior by requiring exclusion of any evidence obtained by state and local law enforcement officials in violation of the Fourth Amendment's prohibition on unreasonable search and seizure.

Building Up and Tearing Down

The twentieth-century reform movement affecting law enforcement organizations and Warren-era Supreme Court decisions mandating rules for police behavior led to greater professionalization of law enforcement agencies and personnel. These changes not only affected the organization and mission of police departments but also resulted in higher qualifications and enhanced training programs for police officers. As a result of these changes, documented reductions in police lawlessness and corruption in urban police departments occurred in the 1960s and thereafter.

Complaints Upheld Against Police

| | | Race of Officer | | |
		Anglo	Latino	Black
Race of Complainant	Anglo	7%	21%	14%
	Latino	5%	8%	8%
	Black	4%	8%	10%

Source: *Los Angeles Times*, May 19, 1991.

Police officials initially decried the expected adverse effects of protecting criminal defendants' rights, and conservative politicians, including officials in the Reagan administration, continually criticized Supreme Court decisions. However, after two decades of experience, many law enforcement officials apparently support *Miranda* warnings, the exclusionary rule, and other judicial limits on police behavior. For example, in a 1986 study of the Chicago Police Department, the head of the Narcotics Section, Commander John Byle, was quoted as saying: "[The exclusionary rule] makes the police department more professional. It enforces appropriate standards of behavior." Similarly, *Miranda* warnings as well as the exclusionary rule have been reported to be "widely credited with improving professionalism among policemen [sic]—and as a result the reforms enjoy growing support among even the most hard-bitten cops." Thus the judicially mandated rules may be regarded as successful in professionalizing police behavior and alleviating many of the abusive practices of the past.

The Supreme Court decisions of the 1980s that loosened the

limits on police behavior have been criticized for creating new risks of abusive practices or, more precisely, creating opportunities to return to abusive practices of the past. When the new Court majority created the "good-faith" exception to the exclusionary rule, the dissenters complained that "the Court's 'reasonable mistake' exception to the exclusionary rule will tend to put a premium on police ignorance of the law." In opposing the creation of a "public safety" exception to *Miranda* warnings, the dissenters asserted that the majority "expressly invit[ed] police officers to coerce defendants into making incriminating statements." In other words, critics of the Court's recent decisions see the relaxed standards as not only violating individuals' constitutional protections but also encouraging regressive developments in the professionalization of police practices. . . .

These policy-based decisions have affected the justices' characterizations of protections for criminal defendants. Warren-era justices who expanded defendants' rights claimed that the protections were mandated by the Constitution, while recent decisions characterize the prior cases as creating judge-made and hence nonbinding, changeable rules.

Opposing Perspectives About Criminal Rights

A second and largely unrecognized influence on recent criminal procedure decisions is the relationship between police professionalization and justices' perceptions of law enforcement practices. Because police made significant strides toward professionalization as a result of the reform movement and the Warren-era decisions, perceptions of the risks of police abuse have apparently diminished in the minds of recent Court appointees. The *Mapp* and *Miranda* decisions in the 1960s were premised on a great need to curb the brutal and coercive tactics commonly employed by law enforcement officials during most of U.S. history. Thus Chief Justice Warren devoted much of his opinion in *Miranda* to chronicling documented abuses by police in seeking to obtain confessions from suspects. Warren and other justices during the 1960s not only remembered the publicity from the Wickersham Commission report in 1931, and other exposés of the 1930s, but also had personal experience with the problems of police misconduct. Chief Justice Warren had observed and even participated in coercive interrogations during his tenure as a prosecuting attorney in California during the 1930s. Justice Douglas had had several unpleasant encounters with local law enforcement officials during his impoverished youth in the early part of this century. . . .

By contrast, four members of the current Court's conservative majority (William H. Rehnquist, Sandra Day O'Connor, Antonin Scalia, and Anthony M. Kennedy) were children during the

1930s and did not reach adulthood until after many abusive police practices had been altered by the reform movement and the Wickersham Commission report. In addition to being oriented toward relaxing rules for police, these justices do not possess the same skepticism about the potential for abuse of police authority as did their predecessors who had personal knowledge of such activities. In effect, the professionalization of police departments and the reduction in blatant abusive practices have dimmed the Supreme Court's institutional memory of the reasons why *Mapp*, *Miranda*, and other Warren-era decisions sought to outline relatively clearly what behavior was acceptable for law enforcement officials. . . .

A Reminder to Police

Whether suspects do not fully grasp the significance of the [Miranda] warnings, or whether conscience (and the desire to get the matter over with) override the impact of the warnings, it is plain that for the past 20 years suspects have continued to confess with great frequency. It is equally plain that this would not have been the case if Miranda really had projected counsel into the police station. . . .

Clearly, the case is an important symbol. But what follows from that? The police should never forget that they do not establish their own interrogation rules and do not police themselves. As Liva Baker, author of "Miranda: Crime, Law and Politics," has pointed out, the warnings "serve a civilizing purpose"—they remind the police officer that however lowly the suspect before him, he is still a human being possessing certain rights.

Yale Kamisar, *The New York Times*, June 11, 1986.

Although the younger justices have apparently been lulled into minimizing the risks of official misbehavior, the question remains whether professionalization, in an era of loosening judicial restrictions, can prevent a return to the coercive practices of the past. In the cases during the 1980s, the Supreme Court endorsed police actions that, intentionally or unintentionally, stretch the boundaries of the Warren-era constitutional protections for criminal defendants. Critics have noted that the Court's recent decisions may encourage law enforcement officials to claim ignorance of facts in order to gain good-faith exceptions to the exclusionary rule; to assert immediate, vague threats to public safety in order to avoid traditional *Miranda* warnings; and even to become lazy to hinder defendants' access to potentially exculpatory evidence without manifesting "bad faith." . . .

In effect, the Warren-era decisions on criminal defendants' rights may have undermined their own foundation by generating police reform and thereby dimming memories of police abuses. Moreover, the residual lessons learned from the Warren era by the professionalized police will likely moderate the level of misconduct and lead to subtle coercive tactics that will not outrage the public, rather than to the blatant brutality of previous decades. Such subtle practices may be no less insidious in their consequences for the protection (or lack thereof) of criminal defendants' constitutional rights. Because the members of the Court's current conservative majority apparently lack any memory of "unprofessional" police conduct that would restrain their crime control policy preferences, future decisions will likely continue to relax requirements for law enforcement officials' conduct. What controls will then be available to prevent official lawlessness? . . .

The immediate future does not look promising for the goal of clarifying and protecting established Fourth, Fifth, and Sixth Amendment rights from intrusion by law enforcement officers. Any increase in police discretion necessarily carries the risk that discretionary authority will be abused. Although the professionalization of law enforcement has altered police practices and generated confidence among younger justices in the trust that can be placed in these public servants, professionalization cannot alter human nature and the political pressures on police to show palpable progress in fighting crime. With a diminished historical perspective evident in the federal judiciary, responsibility for scrutinizing police behavior inevitably will move to interest groups and legal commentators who are relatively powerless to restrain undesirable practices.

For the foreseeable future, the practical burden of maintaining standards of police behavior may fall on law enforcement officials themselves. If, as studies indicate, police officers truly appreciate the professionalizing benefits of *Mapp, Miranda,* and other Warren-era cases, self-restraint may limit the adverse consequences of deteriorating judicial guidelines. There is, however, no reason to expect law enforcement officials to have any greater memory or historical perspective than do current members of the Supreme Court. In fact, political pressures and self-interest inevitably push police officers toward greater experimentation in testing the boundaries of criminal defendants' rights. Unless the Supreme Court regains its institutional memory through such unlikely events as additional changes in the Court's composition or public scandals over police treatment of suspects, subtle coercive practices are likely to grow and spread throughout the law enforcement community.

a critical thinking activity

Recognizing Stereotypes

A stereotype is an oversimplified or exaggerated description of people or things. Stereotyping can be favorable. Most stereotyping, however, tends to be highly uncomplimentary, and, at times, degrading.

Stereotyping grows out of our prejudices. When we stereotype someone, we are prejudging him or her. Consider the following cartoon. The cartoonist uses two stereotypes: one, that blacks are criminals and, two, that police officers are bigots.

"Well, Chief, we didn't actually see him doing anything. But he's Black and was walking real fast."

Part I

The following statements relate to the subject matter in this chapter. Consider each statement carefully. *Mark S for any statement that is an example of stereotyping. Mark N for any statement that is not an example of stereotyping. Mark U if you are undecided about any statement.*

> S = *stereotype*
> N = *not a stereotype*
> U = *undecided*

1. Police officers are altruistic and brave.

2. Black men are too lazy to work.

3. Blacks make up a disproportionate number of America's prison population.

4. Police officers are afraid of being killed in the line of duty.

5. Cops are power-hungry bullies.

6. White police officers have brutalized nonwhite citizens.

7. The police protect and serve citizens.

8. Latino men are very protective of their families.

9. Asian Americans are hard-working, honest people.

10. Many Hispanics live in Southern California.

11. Big cities have more crime than small towns.

12. Police do not care about people's civil rights.

13. Rodney King got what he deserved.

14. Police departments are racist.

Part II

Based on the insights you have gained from this activity, discuss these questions in class:

1. Why do people stereotype one another?

2. What are some examples of positive stereotypes?

3. What harm can stereotypes cause?

4. What stereotypes currently affect members of your class?

Periodical Bibliography

The following articles have been selected to supplement the diverse views presented in this chapter.

Cathy Booth, Edwin M. Reingold, and Elaine Shannon	"Police Brutality!" *Time*, March 25, 1991.
Alexander Cockburn	"Beat the Devil," *The Nation*, April 15, 1991.
Barbara Dority	"Police Powers Expanded as Abuses Escalate," *The Humanist*, July/August 1991.
Joe Foss	"The President's Column," *American Rifleman*, May 1990. Available from 1600 Rhode Island Ave. NW, Washington, DC 20036.
Ted Gest et al.	"Why Brutality Persists," *U.S. News & World Report*, April 1, 1991.
William F. Jasper	"ACLU: The Attack Continues," *The New American*, June 4, 1991. Available from 770 Westhill Blvd., Appleton, WI 54915.
William F. Jasper	"Keep Them Local, Keep Us Free," *The New American*, May 21, 1991.
Murry Kempton	"Cops Ape Style of Criminal They Pursue," *Liberal Opinion Week*, February 10, 1992. Available from 108 E. Fifth St., Vinton, IA 52349.
Jeanne McDowell	"Are Women Better Cops?" *Time*, February 17, 1992.
John McManus	"Support Your Local Police," *The New American*, April 23, 1991.
Micah Morrison	"Cops Get Up-Close and Personal," *Insight*, August 10, 1992. Available from 3600 New York Ave. NE, Washington, DC 20002.
Michael Novick	"Watchdog or Lapdog?" *The Minority Trendsletter*, Spring 1992.
Kayne B. Robinson	"The New Police Peril: Civilian Review Boards," *American Rifleman*, May 1991.
Carl Rowan	"We Must Not Give More Power to America's Police," *Liberal Opinion Week*, July 22, 1991.

Organizations to Contact

The editors have compiled the following list of organizations that are concerned with the issues debated in this book. All have publications or information available for interested readers. For best results, allow as much time as possible for the organizations to respond. The descriptions below are derived from materials provided by the organizations. This was compiled upon the date of publication. Names, addresses, and phone numbers of organizations are subject to change.

American Bar Association (ABA)
Criminal Justice Section
1800 M St. NW, 2d Floor, South Lobby
Washington, DC 20036-5886
(202) 331-2260

Founded in 1921, the American Bar Association's Criminal Justice Section is comprised of attorneys, law students, judges, law professors, and law enforcement personnel interested in the quick, fair, and effective administration of criminal justice. The association has more than twenty committees that address the services and functions of defense attorneys and prosecutors. Publications include the quarterly *Criminal Justice* magazine and various reference books, course materials, and legal analyses.

American Civil Liberties Union (ACLU)
132 W. 43rd St.
New York, NY 10016
(212) 944-9800

The ACLU is one of America's oldest civil liberties organizations. Founded in 1920, the ACLU champions the rights set forth in the Declaration of Independence and the Constitution. The ACLU provides legal defense, research, and education. It publishes the quarterly newspaper *Civil Liberties* and various pamphlets, books, and position papers.

American Criminal Justice Association (ACJA)
PO Box 61047
Sacramento, CA 95860
(916) 484-6553

The ACJA is made up of retired criminal justice professionals, students of criminal justice, and other citizens concerned with criminal justice. The association seeks to improve the professional standards of criminal justice personnel. It publishes the semiannual *Journal of the American Criminal Justice Association*.

American Judicature Society
25 E. Washington St., Suite 1600
Chicago, IL 60602
(312) 558-6900

The society is a group of lawyers, judges, law teachers, government officials, and citizens interested in the effective administration of justice. The society conducts research, offers a consultation service, and works to combat court congestion and delay. It publishes the bimonthly journal *Judicature*.

Americans for Effective Law Enforcement (AELE)
5519 N. Cumberland Ave., No. 1008
Chicago, IL 60656-1471
(312) 763-2800

AELE attempts to help police, prosecutors, and courts promote fairer, more effective administration of criminal law and equal justice for all. Publications include the monthly *Jail and Prison Law Bulletin* and several other regular publications.

Center for Constitutional Rights
666 Broadway, 7th Floor
New York, NY 10012
(212) 614-6464

The center works to halt and reverse what it believes is the erosion of civil liberties in the United States. It specifically targets issues pertaining to the loss of rights during the administration of criminal justice. It publishes the quarterly *Movement Support Network News*.

Center for Law in the Public Interest (CLIPI)
11835 W. Olympic Blvd., Suite 1155
Los Angeles, CA 90064
(213) 470-3000

Founded in 1971, CLIPI is an organization of attorneys who represent groups for free. The center publishes the quarterly *Public Interest Briefs*.

HALT: Americans for Legal Reform
1319 F St. NW, Suite 300
Washington, DC 20004
(202) 347-9600

HALT's goal is to reduce the cost of legal services and to find ways to expedite the litigation process. It believes that many cases can be settled with minimal or no lawyer intervention. Its publications include the monthly newsletter *Frontlines* and the quarterly magazine *The Legal Reformer*.

National Association for Crime Victims Rights (NACVR)
PO Box 16161
Portland, OR 97216-0161
(503) 252-9012

NACVR members are from local businesses, professional groups, and others frustrated with the increase in crime. Through Operation Strike Back, members help victims assert their rights, hold victimization seminars, and sponsor self-defense classes. The association publishes the quarterly *Crimes Eye Newsletter*.

National Association of Blacks in Criminal Justice (NABCJ)
PO Box 9499
Washington, DC 20016-9499
(301) 681-2365

Founded in 1972, this organization is comprised of criminal justice professionals concerned with the impact of criminal justice policies and practices on the minority community. It seeks to increase the influence of blacks in the system. Publications include the quarterly *NABCJ Newsletter*.

National Association of Criminal Defense Lawyers
1627 K St. NW, 12th Floor
Washington, DC 20006
(202) 872-8688

Established in 1958, the association promotes the adversary system of justice, maintains professional standards for defense attorneys, and protects the rights of individuals accused of crimes. It publishes *The Champion* ten times a year.

National Criminal Justice Association
444 N. Capitol St. NW, Suite 608
Washington, DC 20001
(202) 347-4900

The association collects and publishes information on national and state criminal justice issues and developments. Its objectives are to focus attention on crime control, to publish states' views on pending national legislation in areas related to crime, and to improve states' administration of their criminal and juvenile justice systems. The association publishes the monthly *Justice Bulletin*.

National District Attorneys Association (NDAA)
99 Canal Center Plaza, Suite 510
Alexandria, VA 22314
(703) 549-9222

NDAA is an organization comprised of assistant prosecuting attorneys, investigators, paralegals, and other prosecution office staff. The association seeks to improve the administration of justice, especially in the areas of juvenile justice and child abuse. The association publishes *Case Commentaries and Briefs* ten times a year, *NDAA Bulletin* bimonthly, and the *Prosecutor* quarterly.

National Institute for Citizen Education in the Law
711 G St. SE
Washington, DC 20003
(202) 546-6644

This organization educates the American public about the legal system. It conducts student mock trials, teen action programs, and other law-related educational projects to promote knowledge and respect for the law. The institute publishes the semiannual *Street Law News* and various textbooks, teachers' guides, articles, and brochures relating to law.

National Institute of Justice (NIJ)
U.S. Department of Justice
Box 6000
Rockville, MD 20850
(800) 851-3420

The NIJ is a research and development agency that documents crime and its control. It publishes and distributes its information through the National Criminal Justice Reference Service, an international clearinghouse that provides information and research about criminal justice. It publishes the *National Institute of Justice Journal* bimonthly.

National Institute of Victimology
2333 N. Vernon St.
Arlington, VA 22207
(703) 528-3387

Founded in 1976, the institute works to improve victim/witness services and to make the public and criminal justice personnel aware of the needs of crime victims. It publishes *Victimology: An International Journal* quarterly.

National Legal Aid and Defender Association
1625 K St. NW, 8th Floor
Washington, DC 20006
(202) 452-0620

The association provides information, technical support, and management assistance to local organizations that provide legal services for the poor. It publishes the *Capital Report* bimonthly and *Cornerstone* five times a year.

National Organization for Victim Assistance (NOVA)
1757 Park Rd. NW
Washington, DC 20010
(202) 232-6682

NOVA serves as a national forum for victim advocacy by assisting victims of crime, providing education and technical assistance to those who assist victims, and serving as a membership organization for those who support the victims movement. NOVA publishes the monthly *NOVA Newsletter*.

Police Executive Research Forum
2300 M St. NW, Suite 910
Washington, DC 20037
(202) 466-7820

The forum is comprised of executives of large police agencies who seek to educate the public about criminal justice matters. The forum sponsors research and experimentation in criminal justice. The organization's publications include *Problem Solving Quarterly* and the bimonthly *Subject to Debate*.

VERA Institute of Justice
377 Broadway, 11th Floor
New York, NY 10013
(212) 334-1300

VERA conducts research on bail reform, nonpenal approaches to public drunkenness, and other criminal justice issues. It sponsors the Victim/Witness Assistance Project, which provides services to crime victims and witnesses. The institute publishes the semiannual journal *Federal Sentencing Reporter*.

Victims of Crime and Leniency (VOCAL)
PO Box 4449
Montgomery, AL 36103
(205) 262-7197

VOCAL is an organization of crime victims who seek to ensure that their rights are recognized and protected. They believe that the U.S. justice system goes to great lengths to protect the rights of criminals while discounting those of victims. VOCAL publishes the quarterly newsletter *VOCAL Voice*.

Bibliography of Books

Richard L. Abel — *American Lawyers*. New York: Oxford University Press, 1989.

Richard L. Abel and Philip S. C. Lewis, eds. — *Lawyers in Society.* Vol. 3, *Comparative Theories*. Berkeley: University of California Press, 1989.

David Austern — *The Crime Victim's Handbook: Your Rights and Role in the Criminal Justice System*. New York: Viking, 1987.

Douglas J. Besharov, ed. — *Legal Services for the Poor: Time for Reform*. Washington, DC: American Enterprise Institute, 1990.

Mark Blumberg, ed. — *AIDS: The Impact on the Criminal Justice System*. Laurel, MD: American Correctional Association, 1990.

David J. Bodenhamer — *Fair Trial: Rights of the Accused in American History*. New York: Oxford University Press, 1991.

Anthony Bouza — *Police Mystique: An Insider's Look at Cops, Crime, and the Criminal Justice System*. New York: Plenum Press, 1990.

John Braithwaite and Philip Pettit — *Not Just Deserts: A Republican Theory of Criminal Justice*. New York: Oxford University Press, 1990.

Stephen Brophy — *Crime, Justice, and Morals*. Boston: Routledge and Kegan Paul, 1984.

Michael Castleman — *Crime Free: Stop Your Chances of Being Robbed, Raped, Mugged, or Burglarized*. New York: Simon and Schuster, 1984.

Charles Colson and Daniel Van Ness — *Convicted: New Hope for Ending America's Crime Crisis*. Westchester, IL: Crossway Books, 1989.

Elliott Currie — *Confronting Crime*. New York: Pantheon Books, 1985.

Edwin J. Delattre — *Character and Cops: Ethics in Policing*. Washington, DC: American Enterprise Institute, 1989.

Shirley Dicks — *Victims of Crime and Punishment*. Jefferson, NC: McFarland and Co., 1991.

Paula DiPerna — *Juries on Trial: Faces of American Justice*. New York: Dembner Books, 1984.

Frank Donner — *Protectors of Privilege: Red Squads and Police Repression in Urban America*. Berkeley: University of California Press, 1990.

Warren Freedman — *The Constitutional Right to a Speedy and Fair Criminal Trial*. New York: Quorum Books, 1989.

Burt Galaway and Joe Hudson, eds. *Criminal Justice, Restitution, and Reconciliation.* Laurel, MD: American Correctional Association, 1990.

Daryl F. Gates *Chief: My Life in the LAPD.* New York: Bantam Books, 1992.

Robert A. Goldwin and William A. Schambra, eds. *The Constitution, the Courts, and the Quest for Justice.* Washington, DC: American Enterprise Institute, 1989.

Diana R. Gordon *The Justice Juggernaut: Fighting Street Crime, Controlling Citizens.* New Brunswick, NJ: Rutgers University Press, 1990.

Don M. Gottfredson and Ronald V. Clarke, eds. *Policy and Theory in Criminal Justice.* Brookfield, VT: Gower Publishing Co., 1990.

Don M. Gottfredson and Michael Tonry, eds. *Prediction and Classification: Criminal Justice Decision Making.* Vol. 9. Chicago: University of Chicago Press, 1987.

Jack R. Greene and Stephen D. Mastrofski, eds. *Community Policing: Rhetoric or Reality?* New York: Praeger, 1988.

Valerie P. Hans and Neil Vidmar *Judging the Jury.* New York: Plenum Press, 1986.

Bertram Harnett *Law, Lawyers, and Laymen.* San Diego: Harcourt Brace Jovanovich, 1984.

Bruce Jackson *Law and Disorder: Criminal Justice in America.* Bloomington: Indiana University Press, 1985.

Philip J. Jenkins *Crime and Justice: Issues and Ideas.* Monterey, CA: Brooks-Cole, 1984.

Peter E. Kane *Murder, Courts, and the Press: Issues in Free Press/Fair Trial.* Carbondale: Southern Illinois University Press, 1986.

Don B. Kates Jr. *Firearms and Violence.* San Francisco: Pacific Institute for Public Policy Research, 1984.

Saul M. Kassin and Lawrence S. Wrightsman *The American Jury on Trial: Psychological Perspectives.* New York: Hemisphere Publishing Corp., 1988.

Stacey Koon *Presumed Guilty.* Washington, DC: Regnery Gateway, 1992.

William H. Kroes *Society's Victims—The Police: An Analysis of Job Stress in Policing.* Springfield, IL: Charles C. Thomas, 1985.

David Luban *Lawyers and Justice: An Ethical Study.* Princeton, NJ: Princeton University Press, 1988.

Arthur J. Lurigio, Wesley G. Skogan, and Robert C. Davis, eds. *Victims of Crime: Problems, Policies, and Programs.* Newbury Park, CA: Sage Publications, 1990.

| Mark H. McCormack | *The Terrible Truth About Lawyers*. New York: William Morrow, 1987. |

Patrick B. McGuigan and Jon S. Pascale, eds. — *Crime and Punishment in Modern America*. Lanham, MD: University Press of America, 1986.

David W. Marston — *Malice Aforethought*. New York: William Morrow, 1991.

Alfredo Mirandé — *Gringo Justice*. Notre Dame, IN: University of Notre Dame Press, 1987.

Peter F. Nardulli, James Eisenstein, and Roy B. Flemming — *The Tenor of Justice: Criminal Courts and the Guilty Plea Process*. Urbana: University of Illinois Press, 1988.

Richard A. Posner — *The Federal Courts: Crisis and Reform*. Cambridge, MA: Harvard University Press, 1985.

Jeffrey H. Reiman — *The Rich Get Richer and the Poor Get Prison: Ideology, Class, and Criminal Justice*. New York: Wiley & Sons, 1984.

Gerald N. Rosenberg — *The Hollow Hope: Can Courts Bring About Social Change?* Chicago: University of Chicago Press, 1991.

Stanley E. Rosenblatt — *Trial Lawyer*. Secaucus, NJ: Lyle Stuart, 1984.

Edgardo Rotman — *Beyond Punishment: A New View on the Rehabilitation of Criminal Offenders*. Westport, CT: Greenwood Press, 1990.

Wesley G. Skogan — *Disorder and Decline: Crime and the Spiral of Decay in American Neighborhoods*. New York: The Free Press, 1990.

Jerome H. Skolnick and David H. Bayley — *The New Blue Line: Police Innovation in Six American Cities*. New York: The Free Press, 1986.

Steven Rathgeb Smith and Susan Freinkel — *Adjusting the Balance: Federal Policy and Victim Services*. Westport, CT: Greenwood Press, 1988.

Michael Tonry and Norval Morris, eds. — *Crime and Justice: A Review of Research*. Vol. 10. Chicago: University of Chicago Press, 1988.

Michael Tonry and Norval Morris, eds. — *Modern Policing*. Chicago: University of Chicago Press, 1991.

Eugene D. Wheeler and Robert E. Kallman — *Stop Justice Abuse*. Ventura, CA: Pathfinder Press, 1986.

William Wilbanks — *The Myth of a Racist Criminal Justice System*. Monterey, CA: Brooks-Cole, 1987.

James Q. Wilson and Richard J. Herrnstein — *Crime and Human Nature*. New York: Simon and Schuster, 1985.

Seymour Wishman — *Anatomy of a Jury*. New York: Times Books, 1986.

Index

209

211